THE ROAD TO
KEY WEST

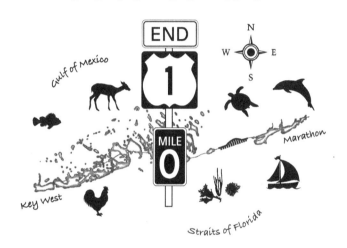

MARATHON TO KEY WEST

The guide every local should have for their guest
and every visitor should have by their side

by Brian Branigan

ISBN: 978-0-9892840-1-1

Written by Brian Branigan
Photography by Brian Branigan
Design by Allison Culbertson

Contact info:
Email: info@theroadtokeywest.com
Website: theroadtokeywest.com
To Advertise: 305-699-7166

Printed in the United States of America

Visit Us Online:
TheRoadToKeyWest.com
IslandDesign.us – graphic & web design
KeysBoatTours.com – eco, snorkel, fish, paddle, sandbar, & lessons

Partial proceeds from this book go to Op/Prop, aka "Operation Propagule." A propagule is living fruit from the red mangrove tree. Our goal is to help encourage the growth of the damaged mangrove islands from Hurricane Irma. It is modeled after similar coral reef restoration projects. Read more about this effort in back pages of the book. Thank you for your purchase.

Dedicated to all essential workers, especially hospital staff.
Thank you for helping us get through a very difficult time.
We owe you our life.

And, to all natural disaster victims, emergency response personnel,
and helpful friends and strangers who rise to the occasion when
the need occurs. Thank you!

Dear Mom,

My vacation to the FL Keys has taken a turn - I have decided to stay.

Unexpected, I know, but this is the right place for me at this time - good people, nature, and warmth. I can be creative, healthy and employed.

It's just too crazy on the mainland. And, those winters!!

I hope that you can visit soon.

POST CARD

You never know, you might want to stay too.
Love always,
Allison

PS: You have to try this amazing key lime pie recipe in the back of this great little book! XO

PLACE STAMP HERE

Postcard by IslandDesign.us ©2019

IslandDesign

Greetings from the Florida Keys:

To: _____

From: _____

Old Bahia Honda Railroad Bridge
Scout Key, MM 35

WELCOME TO THE KEYS!

The Road To Key West guarantees to maximize your Keys vacation visit.

It is a locals perspective offering up-to-date information for your Lower Keys: Marathon to Key West visit. It also makes mention of several points of interest above Marathon: **Snappers Oceanfront Restaurant** in Key Largo, **Robbie's** (feed tarpon), **Blond Giraffe** (key lime pie), **Theater Of The Sea**, and **Hideaway Cafe** – to name a few.

The previous installment of this book was updated just after hurricane Irma, in 2017. A lot has changed since then – not all good: political division, pandemic, global warming, inflation, war, and seemingly endless hardship for many. Fortunately, the Keys is a respite from all things negative. We want your Keys visit to be as special as you can make it.

Many Keys businesses have soared during Covid. But, many others have been silenced. Restaurants and bars were hit particularly hard. Thank you for your support, patience, and generosity while patronizing local establishments. Outdoor activities including RV camping, fishing, snorkeling, and paddling have fared far better. But, they too need your support. If you can, during your visit, please eat too much, drink too much, and spend too much – if only for the sake of the economy.

We hope you that you find this book indispensable. It is born of first hand knowledge, pounding the pavement, visiting places, seeing who is still in business, and tasting and sipping tirelessly – all to benefit you and yours. Additional information is grabbed off social media, recommendations for soon-to-be Keys visitors who seek answers: where to bring kids, a good chiropractor, best happy hour, places to eat, music venues, and who to get on the water with.

The questions and answers keep coming – daily. Some local Facebook pages are intended to buy and sell only, while others offer travel and food tips. As an example, see *facebook.com/BigPine/Marathon, facebook.com/whatshappeninginmarathon*, and *facebook.com/keywestyardsale*, As you can imagine, there are many facebook pages for the Keys.

Here are some typical Q&A's re: travel advice on Facebook that you might find particularly helpful for your visit.

Q: Staying in Marathon. Any places to rent or buy snorkeling gear and fishing rods that won't break the bank?

A: **The Tackle Box** on Marathon – they share catch spots too!

A: **Looe Key Dive Center** rents /sells snorkel gear, wetsuits, etc.

A: **Keys Boat Tours** rents and sells snorkel gear at MM 33 at Big Pine Key Resort. Rent for just $15 per 24hr. They have some kayaks and paddleboards too

A: **Divers Direct**, Key West

Q: Turtle Hospital or Aquarium Encounters?

A: Both

A: **Turtle Hospital**

A: **Aquarium Encounters**

A: Don't rule out **Crane Point Hammock.** Great nature trail!

Q: Wondering where to buy local seafood around Marathon?

A: **King Seafood, Keys Fisheries, Brutus** – Marathon

A: The best is **King Seafood** – incredible tuna ceviche appetizer

A: **Brutus Seafood** – Marathon – A good restaurant too!

A: When in season, **Paradise Lobster** – Marathon

A: **Low Key Fisheries** – Cudjoe Key

A: **Generations Seafood Market** – (live lobster) Big Pine Key

Q: How can my family get to the reef without breaking the bank?

A: **Looe Key Reef Resort** dive center on Ramrod Key MM 28

A: **Captain Hooks** on Big Pine at MM 29 – Looe Key

A: **Bahia Honda State Park** MM 36.5 – Looe Key

A: **Marathon Lady** (day and night fishing) good time catching, and affordable, pick a transom spot

A: **Spirit Snorkeling** out of Marathon – Sombrero Lighthouse

A: **Marathon Mermaid** is a great sunset / sandbar boat for many

Q: What are must-dos when traveling from Miami to Key West?

A: **John Pennekamp State Park**, **Keys Brewing Company** (good for kids too), **Robbie's** (feed the tarpon), **Curry Hammock State Park**, **Aquarium Encounters**, **Sunset Grill**, **The 7 Mile Bridge** (enjoy the view but drive carefully), **Bahia Honda State Park** (nice beach), **Sweet Savannah's** baked goods on Marathon, **No Name Pub** (don't feed the Key deer), **Tonio's** on Summerland Key, and in Key West, **Fort Zachary Taylor State Park**

A: Pay attention to the road, don't drink and drive, go the speed limit, and watch out for other drivers who don't follow the must-do rules. Arrive Alive, Leave Alive – and don't kill anyone!

A: **Lazy Days** in Islamorada, tables on the beach. We love **Skippers Dockside** and **Snapper's** too – both in Key Largo. And, **Key Largo Fisheries**. Definitely try **Bongo's Cafe** on the lagoon at Grassy Key.

A: **Keys Boat Tours** MM 33 for: eco, snorkel, and dinner catching – great people! They are rated #1 on TripAdvisor. Captain Brian is the only hands-on motor boat instructor in the entire Keys. He's a great fishing teacher too. Kids love him.

A: **Fort Zach** is way better for sunset than **Mallory Square**, IMO

A: MM 10 left at Shell station, go to **Geiger Key Marina** for lunch, an amazing hide-away right on the water, with a sunset view too.

A: **Dry Tortugas** snorkeling tour. If you can, go by seaplane!

Q: **Any advice on places to eat in and around Marathon please?**

A: **Castaways** (sushi) rustic Keys atmosphere, **Burdines** for a burger and taco salad, **Frank's Grill** (great Italian), **Lazy Days** (water views and good reviews), **Florida Keys Steak and Lobster House**, people love it. **Driftwood** pizza, **Keys Fisheries** upstairs raw bar 21+. Check out **Dockside Bar and Grill** for an eye opening Keysz introduction, and **Overseas Pub** too. **Irie Island Eats** (food truck) inside fruit stand across from Home Depot. And, **Herbie's Bar & Chowder House** is a favorite. If looking for upscale, **Mahina** at Isla Bella, **Butterfly Cafe** at Tranquility Bay, and **Hideaway Cafe** on Grassy Key.

A: I second **Keys Fisheries**, great raw bar and views upstairs. The downstairs is a bit more touristy for casual family dining.

A: Two Marathon favorites: **Sparky's Landing** and **Havana Jacks**.

A: **The Stuffed Pig** is a great breakfast spot with outdoor dining.

Q: **We are in the Lower Keys for a week. Can anyone recommend a reliable boat rental place. And, someone who can help us with navigation tips?**

A: **Captain Pips** – Marathon

A: **Vacation Boat Rentals** – Marathon

A: Captain Brian at **Keys Boat Tours** for hands-on boat lessons and navigation tips, *boatfishlive.net* and *keysboattours.com*

A: Sugarloaf Marina, big pontoon boats, tracks on the GPS. Or, take a boat tour to Marvin Keys from Sugarloaf Marina.

A: Aqua Boat Rentals – Summerland Key, 305-849-4498

A: Captain Brian: We loved our boat lesson! He also offers tours; snorkeling, fishing, and eco tours to name a few. He guides you in the water, and takes great photos too!

Q: Long weekend in the Lower Keys, staying at Big Pine Key Resort MM 33, what to do – Go!

A: Check out **Bahia Honda State Park**, **No Name Pub**, **Boondocks** restaurant – great food, great beer and ½ off happy hour selections on weekdays. Also, a nice gift shop, and live music. **Horseshoe** swimming hole at MM 35 on Scout Key. PS: Google calls it Horseshoe Beach, but there is no beach. **Five Brothers Two** at MM 27 for good Cuban food, Cuban coffee, and fresh seafood market. Try the **Square Grouper** restaurant on Cudjoe Key. And, also on Cudjoe Key, **Broil** *"Small Island Steakhouse"*

A: Crane Point Museum and Nature Center in Marathon

A: Go to **Pigeon Key**, ferry or private boat $15 fee per person

A: S.S. Wreck & Galley Grill, next to the **Dolphin Research Center**

A: Bahia Honda State Park. Keep it local and check out the Key deer on Big Pine Key, and the **No Name Pub** too. Also, **Marathon** is super close (just 7 miles over the bridge) for good restaurants, music, etc. Check out **Barnacle Barney's Tiki Bar** at Blue Green Vacation Hammocks for their sunset celebration.

A: Big Pine Key Flea Market – Open Sat and Sun 8AM -2PM

A: Those are all great suggestions. Enjoy!

A: FYI: I just discovered the **ResortPass** app that for $25+ you can reserve a day pass, cabana, day room, pool in several resorts in KW and Marathon. This is the way to go if you are staying in eg; Marathon but want to spend the day in Key West, and have the convenience to shower and change for dinner later.

Q: Coming to the Keys for a healthy retreat. Suggestions?

A: I'd rather die, LOL

A: Ha!

A: The Keys: a drinking place with a fishing problem

A: Don't be so cynical guys, it is possible

A: Totally possible: smoothie and fresh fruit for breakfast, great five mile walks or 6 to 12 mile bike ride – 4 days a week. Add some light stretching and exercises into the mix, then take a dip at a swimming hole, maybe do some relaxing laps. Enjoy a clean lunch, fish or chicken over salad, crash a resort and make it yours for an hour or so, read **Hemingway**, or **Hiaasen**. Stay away from bread, beer, and junk food. It's only two weeks! Or, maybe just 2 short months. Up to you. I might offer this as a retreat vacation, and even include housing, if anyone is interested that is.

A: I am interested

A: Me too, just PM'ed you

Q: Heading to Key West for two nights. Any recommendations?

A: If a special occasion, reserve a lunch or dinner at **Latitudes** restaurant on **Sunset Key**. The ferry is free and the food is great. Enjoy a stroll on their beach too

A: **Butterfly Conservatory**, **Hemingway Home**, **Truman Annex** and **Eco Discovery Museum**, **Blue Heaven** restaurant, bar hop, **Pepe's** or **Harpoon Harry's** for breakfast. Rest your feet in hotel lobbies. If you can, a schooner sail at sunset. And, enjoy the great architecture and exotic flora off Duval Street in Old Town

A: **Fort Zach** inside **Truman Annex** to beach and sunset, **Green Parrot Bar** for music, **Hank's Saloon** for music and **Garbo's Grill** food truck, **B.O.'s Fish Wagon**, Happy hour at **Two Friends** or **Half Shell Raw Bar**. **Viva Argentina Steak House**, **A&B Lobster House**, and **Onlywood**, all great dinner spots

A: **La Te Da** for drinks, and afterward – a drag show at La Te Da, or at **Aqua Bar**!

A: **Kermit's Key West Key Lime Pie Shoppe**, Also, try the towering key lime pie at **Blue Heaven** – share a slice

A: I definitely recommend an overnight stay during your visit to Key West. Also, rent a bike rather than pound the pavement, but follow traffic rules. Check out the boats along the boardwalk at **Conch Harbor Marina**, And, the back streets off of Duval too, like Southard and Grinnell streets, where you'll find **Five Brothers**: Cuban coffee, sandwiches, and eclairs. Go to the cemetery too. Then, **Thai Island** restaurant for sushi and curry.

A: **Mallory Square** is for sunset, if only once, I liked the aquarium too, small but fun, Go to **Sloppy Joe's** for a beer and music, **Books & Books**, And, **Santiago's Bodega** (tapas), **El Siboney** (Cuban food), **Hogfish Bar** on Stock Island (Safe Harbor Marina). Check out the pool at the college too, Just $5 to swim laps. And if you like golf, a very fun golf course across the way

Q: What is the customary tip for fishing and snorkeling guides?

A: Glad you used the word customary. The short answer is 20%

A: There are captains and first mates. This is a lifetime experience for you. Be as generous as possible, mates get paid from tips, so 20% per outing. Then, throw the Capt $100.

A: I mean, if he or she puts you on the fish and works hard, reward them properly at least 20%. Don't play dumb and tip $20 or $50.

A: I once went out with a charter captain and got skunked. Afterward, he complained that I didn't tip enough. Is that normal?

A: Hey, don't forget wait staff: at least 20%. Make their day or night with a $100 tip. It will make your day too.

A: I remember my best tip ever as a server, $500. I couldn't believe it at the time. It still feels like a dream.

A: If you tip less that 20% expect the captain, mate, server, or whoever to question you about it. Tips are key to overall wages.

A: You should never get skunked with the right captain - never!

Q: Best exercise bike rides and walk places in the Lower Keys?

A: Old Seven Mile Bridge, Marathon to Pigeon Key. Park at the bridge MM 47. Approx 5 miles roundtrip. Spectacular views!

A: Big Pine Key, MM 33, oceanside, Long Beach Road, very scenic, Key deer, ocean views, great workout. Five mile roundtrip.

A: Big Pine Key (at the traffic light), Key Deer Blvd., bay side. Go up KDB on the walk / bike path to the Blue Hole, resident alligator. Roud trip is 5 miles. Or, up KDB to Watson, go right to end, then left to end of No Name Key and back, 10 miles. You can also bike and hike this route too. Near the end of No Name Key on the right, **Paradise Trial**, See it on the **All Trails** app. Trail is only good for hiking during rain free weeks.

A: Summerland Key and Cudjoe Key, aka **Tonio's** restaurant to **Mangrove Mama's**. You can bike and or walk (on the path) almost the entire four miles each way. Or, just start at **Ace Hardware** on Summerland Key. Cross US 1 to **Old State Road 4A** (path) to end 0.8 mile each way, Or, cross US 1 again, and continue over the fishing bridge to Cudjoe Key and back, for a 3 mile bike or hike.

A: We love Sugarloaf Blvd. Park at **Sugarloaf Lodge**, MM 17. Cross US 1 and go 2.6 miles each way to the turn, or 5.5 miles. Or, perhaps best of all, drive down to the turn; turn and park (past the no parking signs). Then walk back to the turn and trailhead which is **Loop Road**. This pedestrian only 4 mile loop is breathtaking. Afterward, consider a leap from the jumping bridge, the first bridge you cross. Or, just take in the spectacular views there. This is a great place for a picnic too. Two miles further down the road (past where you parked) is **Sammy's Point** and kayak launch - very special. Also, check out *discoverybicycletours.com/floridakeys/multiadventure*

Q: I am motion sensitive. Where are the best fishing bridges?

A: MM 40 Old Seven Mile Bridge. Park at the boat ramp

A: Spanish Harbor boat ramp, MM 33.5, bay side.

A: MM 30, connecting Big Pine Key to No Name Key, the Old Wooden Bridge. Unload your gear then park on either side of bridge.

A: MM 21, ocean side, where Summerland Key meets Cudjoe Key, Kemp Channel fishing bridge. Parking available.

A: If you are in need of a guide, or desire lessons on how to fish from a bridge, contact Ryan and **LandBoat Charters**, 305-204-9772 and *fishthebridges.com* Note: a fishing license is required when fishing off of a bridge.

Q: Best swimming holes?

A: Can't reveal. Locals will never forgive me.

A: We can tell them one, no?

A: OK, one; MM 35, bay side, **Horseshoe** swimming hole, on Scout Key / bay side. Last left going toward Miami, 1st right going to KW.

A: One more: the pool at College of the FL Keys, Stock Island MM 5, turn at the Hospital.

Q: What are five great restaurants worthy of a special occasion?

A: Hideaway Cafe on Grassy Key

A: Butterfly Cafe at **Tranquility Bay** Resort, Marathon

A: Broil *"Small island steakhouse"* on Cudjoe Key

A: Little Pearl in Key West. Also, **A&B Lobster House**

A: Latitudes in Key West on Sunset Key (includes a boat ride).

A: Beware the $40 entree and $15 glass of wine – the new norm

Of course, there is a constructive side and a cynical side to social media, and Keys people too. And, different strokes for different folks, but we knew that. Take the best of these Q&A's and apply them to your visit. The suggestions made in these Facebook exchanges might be all that you need. Streamline a list that's right for you, and have a great time with it.

The goal of this book is help you secure a positive impression of the Florida Keys. But first, learn some history of the place. In the case of the Keys: the reef, coral, and Henry Flagler. This isn't Machu Picchu, but it is does have a rich and interesting back story. A few suggestions for good reads include; **Last Train To Paradise, The Florida Keys: A History Of The Pioneers**, and Hemingway's, **To Have And Have Not.**

There are all types of people in the Keys. Some come for the bars, and others for the stars – at night. Some are social butterflies and others look for an escape, even liking the idea of being dropped off on a deserted island with nothing more than a tent and some rations. We have backcountry fly fishermen and woman, and offshore sport fishermen and woman. Many come to fulfill their bucket list dreams, while others simply want to grab some relaxation and catch a tan. You might wish to snorkel, and see the many beautiful colorful fish that live here.

There is something for everyone, except perhaps Caribbean like beaches. If that is your hope, you might be slightly disappointed. The barrier reef, four miles offshore is just that – a barrier. It prevents waves from forming, and shells from breaking to create sand beaches. We do have beaches, in Marathon, Key West, and at resorts – and they are nice. But, what is perhaps even more special is the Keys backcountry islands; lagoons, and low tide sandbars that seem to stretch on forever, some of which are nothing short of magical – with great birdlife too. To experience these, I suggest a tour out of Sugarloaf Marina, and some out of Key West, but during low tide (in the backcountry that is) as tides vary.

Paradise like life, is not always dreamy. In the case of the Keys, we have hurricanes. Fortunately, they are relatively few and far between, especially – direct hits. Fortunate too, perhaps is the advance notice we get with hurricanes via technology, unlike tornados, flash floods, and some wildfires. So, we are thankful for that. But, when the big one does hit – it is often a months long or years long event, and a financial reckoning. There is a certain art to living an affordable life in the Keys. But, after a hurricane occurs you are left to ponder, *"Do I have a lot of irons in the fire, or too many eggs in one basket?"* The road back is long and hard.

Then, there are the unnatural challenges, the ones like, *"How do I cover expenses on minimum wage?"* It is why businesses find it difficult to hire people who can stay on for more than a season, much less a year. It has been this way long before Covid, always with the promise of affordable housing. But, the term affordable is likely $2500 per month plus utilities. As generous as people might think $15 per hour is – it isn't.

So, paradise? Many visitors think so, especially those who dream of a re-visit to the Keys. It is what keeps them going – the thought of return. Many longtime residents think of the Keys as paradise too, even if they have to work a couple of minimum wage jobs to keep a roof over their heads. And, even if they haven't been on the water in years – the reason they moved to the Keys in the first place. Reality got in the way, but they still love it. *"We are all here because we are not all there"* someone once said, I think it was at Coconuts bar on Big Pine Key. In any case, how you choose your lifestyle is what truly makes a place paradise, or not.

If you can, please pay your good fortune forward. A stranger treated me to a cafe con leche one day – out of the blue. She just told the cashier, I am paying for his too. I said, I'll cover the tip. It made my day. Let us not forget, that at the height of Covid, it was the front line workers who got paid the least, hospital staff and service industry folk, who did the most, risking their lives so that we all could get groceries, take-out food, fuel, basic necessities, and care for our loved ones. These minimum wage *"essential workers"* were proclaimed heros for a time, but in truth, their reward was only to keep their jobs, put food on the table, and early access to the vaccine. Hardly a reward. So, please do what you can.

The server who just brought you that amazing meal, she lives in a studio apartment for $2500 per month – a deal. She works six days per week. Her savings is small. The original dream? To get her captain's license, buy a sailboat, and sail the Caribbean. Afterward, maybe offer tours for hire. She came to the Keys, and got a job. It was all coming together. Then, Covid happened. Dream dashed. The dream now? Start over, get a roommate to help pay rent, build up savings again, and hope-fully, sooner than later, buy that boat. At least the dream is still alive.

The tour captain who was out of work for a year due to hurricane Irma, he likes to bring people in front the $1M+ beach homes on Big Pine Key. He stops and says, *"This is where we live, Big Pine Key. You see the eighth house over, the one painted white with the red roof? It has palm trees around it with a dock and a tiki hut over the filet station."* He then counts aloud so to give his passengers time to take it in: *"one, two, three, four, five, six, seven, eight."* He hears a whispered *"Wow"*, to which he responds, *"We live two miles behind that in a mobile home."*

It generally gets a good laugh, mostly because it is true. Good humor derives from truth, something we can all relate to.

This same charter captain, who feels fortunate to still be in business, completed a full renovation of his mobile home just two weeks before hurricane Irma hit. Brand new appliances, new beds still in their boxes, and even a collection art work on the floor below where they were to be hanged – ruined. One year and minus $60K later, back in business. But, it took 4 years to eventually break even. Fortunately, he had a live-aboard boat during the first renovation that survived the storm. It provided much needed shelter for the second months-long renovation.

For every natural disaster, there is the other side of the coin: fresh growth and nutrients, forced change, a revived economy, and federal dollars for infrastructure programs. That is the hope. In the case of the charter captain, he benefitted from a HUD program, Rebuild Florida. His mobile home was purposely demolished four years after the storm and replaced with an elevated two bed, two bath home – free of charge. He considers himself – nothing short of a lottery winner, especially with so many disasters since Irma. Disasters seem so common nowadays that a fatigue has set in. But, we can never tire of helping others.

We can all agree that hardships such as the California wildfires, the northwest heatwaves, properties lost, drought, sudden freezes, earthquakes, Kentucky tornados, Colorado fires, and the freak floods in New Jersey, Germany, Tennessee, and elsewhere are incredibly heartbreaking. One only hopes that it is a giant wake up call to address global warming. Harder still, that these events happened on the heels of a pandemic. It is almost too much to bare. But, how lucky are we to be in a place to take our minds off hardship, the fabulous Florida Keys? And, we deserve it.

Did you happen to fly into Key West and look down at the archipelago below? There is so little land relative to the surrounding waters, I sometimes think that we are a little crazy to live here. Even so, it has been years since we have traveled out of the Keys by road. We don't call it a vacation, but instead, an evacuation. That is the only time that we find ourselves on the mainland – to evacuate an approaching storm. The last time we visited Miami? That would be 2009.

People often ask, *"Is it because you love the Keys so much?"* My generally response is, *"No, it's because I work so much."* You will hear that a lot in the Keys, mostly from people who need the money, but also from people who have a difficult time turning down good pay, like a $650+ charter. It is rewarding to make a living on the water, but it too can feel like work at times. The secret? Stay job fit: fishing fit, snorkel fit, etc. You laugh, but it is true. You have to turn down jobs every now and then to get some rest. It is my advice to all entrepreneurs, but especially to aspiring captains – stay mind and body fit. Your clients will enjoy you more.

Captain, the most common first name in all of the Keys, and for good reason. We are surrounded by seas. Your server – a captain. The bartender, in case your forget his or her name – Captain. Your mechanic, Captain. The local college has a course on being a captain. You might even be here for the sole purpose to become a captain. So, be sure to get on the water during your visit. It is rare that two seas meet as they do here, separated a single road, US 1, along the 113 mile long archipelago. To the north is the gulf, or bay. To the south is the ocean, or Florida Straits. To avoid any confusion, we will refer to it as locals do, not left or right, but bay side and ocean side, much the same as port and starboard.

Then, there is the reef, the only living coral barrier reef in the continental United States, and the third largest reef in the world. It is why Congress enacted a law in 1990 proclaiming the entire Florida Keys a sanctuary - the reef. It is akin to a rain forest, but underwater. 25% of all marine life depend on it. Coral is very particular about where it lives. We feel extremely fortunate to have the right conditions for coral to grow here: clean, shallow, warm, salty, sediment free water. Then, there is the gulf stream current and its constant surface temperature of 80°. It helps keep the water cooler in summer months, and warmer in winter months.

US 1, the main road in the Keys, aka the Overseas Highway, is measured by mile markers (MM), descending from MM 113 above Key Largo, to MM 0 in Key West. This itinerary heads in the direction of Marathon to Key West. Even though many people say north / south, if you are heading to Key West, you are traveling west, with the occasional jog to the north, like on Big Pine Key (at the curve).

The book will now transition to a mile marker journey, starting at MM 50+ in Marathon, then over the Seven Mile Bridge, through the Lower Keys, to MM 0 in Key West. You will need a lot of time to cover all of the information that this little book provides. It may be small, but it is mighty. If you have to make a return trip or two to complete the task – we understand. Some folks come and never leave. But, I digress.

MARATHON

Marathon, a city comprised of 13 islands in the middle Keys often gets overlooked, and understandably so – it is at a major transition point. After all, there is the famous Seven Mile Bridge you are about to go over, best viewed during daylight. There is Key West and the excitement of getting there. And, the best part of the Keys some might argue, the Lower Keys. But, Marathon has undergone a major resurgence in recent years, including the newly restored old railroad bridge to Pigeon Key. It took $40M+ and four years, but it is sure to pay for itself.

Granted, altogether different from Key West, Marathon offers a variety of things to do and places to stay. Impressive hotels and resorts the likes of **Tranquility Bay Beachfront Hotel & Resort**, and the stunning **Isla Bella Beach Resort** – a lush tropical getaway with ocean views. Visit the **Isla Bella Marketplace** cafe whether as a guest, or as a meeting place. There is **Crane Point** – a tropical forest, bird-rescue center, natural history museum, and butterfly conservatory. There is the **Dolphin Research Center**, **Aquarium Encounters**, a **biplane** and **helicopter** rides, and the **Turtle Hospital** to tour – all must do's.

There are several beaches to choose from: **Curry Hammock State Park**, **Coco Plumb** and **Sombrero Beach**. Curry Hammock is a great place to paddle a mangrove tunnel, grassy flats, sandbars, and open ocean. Coco Plumb and Sombrero Beach are dog friendly.

Marathon offers some excellent offshore fishing guides: **High Caliber Fishing Charters**, **Big Game Sportfishing**, and **Main Attraction Sportfishing** to name few. You will not be disappointed, but book early.

Annual festivities include the **Seafood Festival** and the **Seven Mile Bridge Run**. So, don't be too quick to overlook Marathon. Spend a few nights here, a couple of nights in between, like at **Little Torch Cottages** or **Parmer's Resort**. And, then a couple of nights in Key West.

WHERE TO EAT

Marathon has several good places to eat, including **Castaway Waterfront Restaurant & Sushi Bar**, south just off 15th Street. **Burdines Waterfront** is just a tad further down 15th St. There is **Sparky's Landing**, great for its water view and wood fired pizza. **Marathon Grill & Ale House**, **Herbie's Bar & Chowder House** and **Keys Fisheries** are all big favorites. **Overseas Pub & Grill**, and **Dockside** (live music) will introduce you to the *Bloodline* feel of the Keys – but in a good way.

People love **Havana Jack's** in Key Colony Beach. **Lazy Days South**, and **Florida Keys Steak & Lobster House** are very popular too. For great Italian, try **Frank's Grill**. For higher end but worthwhile, **Mahina** at Isla Bella Beach Resort, **Butterfly Cafe** at Tranquility Bay, **and Hideaway Cafe** on Grassy Key. Also, **Sunset Grille,** located at the base of the Seven Mile Bridge – has a bar, grill, pool, and yes – a sunset view.

Turtle Hospital, Marathon, MM 48½

SEVEN MILE BRIDGE

The **Seven Mile Bridge**, MM 47 – the Gulf of Mexico *(bay side)* is to your right, or north. The Straits of Florida *(ocean side)* is to your left. The Florida Straits direction is south. You are driving west. But first, get Keys baptized – take a break at the 7 **Mile Grill**. The Seven Mile Bridge is the gateway to the Lower Keys. The (Old) Seven Mile bridge has undergone major construction at great expense. Enjoy the newly refurbished walk and bike bridge to **Pigeon Key**. Designated as a National Historic Landmark in 1990, Pigeon Key is a former settlement for railroad workers dating to the very early 1900's. It is now used for tours and marine science education programs. You can get there by ferry from **Faro Blanco Marina** at **The Hyatt**. Or, park and then walk or bike.

Bicycles rule in the Keys. But, you will truly appreciate a geared bike when confronted with a stiff head wind. It might be easy getting there but twice as difficult to get back. It is advised to carry water, a long sleeved shirt, sunglasses, a hat, and sunscreen wherever you go. These five top the list. The sun is deceptively strong, especially near an ocean breeze, and will attack a pale complexion in no time. The sun is blinding too, and the thirst *(and chill)* can creep up on you, so best be prepared, e.g., take note of how guides cover up – head to toe, especially in summer months. Then again, the gumbo limbo tree, native to the Keys, is known as the tourist tree due to its red and peeling bark. Up to you.

Another tree, midway out on the Old Seven Mile Bridge is affectionately called **Fred**. Fred has his own Facebook page, and even his own children's book called, **Fred The Tree**. Come December, an adventurous crew scale the bridge each year to decorate Fred with solar powered lights. It definitely cheers things up during holiday season. Thanks crew!

THE OLD HIGHWAY

I would be remiss if I did not mention of the Overseas Railroad (1912-1935), the extension of the Florida East Coast Railway to Key West. Described as The Eighth Wonder of the World, it was the brainchild of Henry Flagler, oil tycoon and industrialist. The railroad required many engineering innovations to connect the archipelago, as well as vast amounts of labor and money. Completed in 1912, it was recognized as a major achievement. The railroad met its end with the Labor Day hurricane of 1935 – the most intense hurricane ever to hit the Keys. The surge swept over the islands and portions of the railroad were severely damaged and destroyed. A tidal wave killed hundreds of the workers and their families. The rescue train did not reach them in time.

Too costly to repair, the railroad and bridges were widened to accept cars traveling in both directions, hence the Overseas Railroad became

the Overseas Highway. aka The Old Highway. It was a temporary fix that lasted nearly forty years, 1939-1978.

Today, many of the old bridges are condemned due to rust and instability of the overhang – rusted I-beams and the concrete it can no longer support above. Some of the bridges were modified into fishing bridges, only achieved by cutting off the overhang back to its original width, and installing new railings at considerable expense.

Old Seven Mile Bridge, Restored fishing bridge, MM 40

You will notice this on the west end of the Old Seven Mile Bridge. Conversely, you will see that the Bahia Honda Rail Bridge, between Bahia Honda Key and Scout Key, is literally falling down. One day perhaps, when the federal government comes through with demolition funds, it will likely be dismantled and become an artificial reef. The new highway was completed from 1978-1982.

The bridges were so narrow, that when two buses confronted one another, both would come to a stop. The drivers would step outside to fold in their side view mirrors. The passengers were in awe, including me in 1975, if not a tad concerned of the entire goings-on. One bus would pass while the other stood still, clearing by inches. The mirrors would then be opened back up, and the respective journeys would continue.

THE LOWER KEYS

A first stop on the southwest side of the Seven Mile Bridge is **Veteran's Memorial Park** and beach – MM 40. Veteran's Beach offers a lovely vista at low tide. The shallow water seems as if one could walk for miles into the sea, so have your wet shoes available. A smart purchase when visiting the FL Keys – wet shoes. Also, while you're at it, buy a long sleeved UPF sun shirt, and a dive shirt too *(rash guard)*. They will protect you from burn, sting, and keep you warm when snorkeling. A *Buff* or neck gaiter, is also advised. One secret about this beach – even though it is calf deep most everywhere, when you go to the west end of the

Veteran's Memorial Park, MM 40, knee deep pathway

Bahia
Honda
Overlook
Bahia
Honda
State
Park,
MM 37

beach, you can literally
dive in from shore. It is what is referred to as
a bomb hole. It is deep enough to dive into but don't – jump instead.
You are sure to surprise a person or two with a great disappearing act.

There are many great guides to get you on the water, some renowned
even who will take you out to fish for tarpon, bonefish, and permit.
Capt. Tim Carlile out of Sugarloaf Marina, *fishsugarloafkey.com*, and
Capt. Gabe Nyblad at *tailchasincharters.com* come to mind. **Keys Boat
Tours** will help you and your family catch dinner, and give you some
good recipes too. For fishing on a budget, perhaps there is no better deal
in the Keys than on **Yankee Capts**, departing out of Safe Harbour Marina on Stock Island for 2, 3, and 4 day trips, *yankeecapts.com*. For an all
but guaranteed catch, call **Capt. Jimmy Gagliardini** and **High Caliber
Fishing Charters** at 305-395-0915. For good videos about kayak fishing in the Keys, go to *youtube.com/keywestkayakfishing*.

Bahia Honda State Park

A visit to **Bahia Honda State Park**, pronounced *"baya-honda"*, is always
recommended. If you can, get a reservation to camp there, or better still,
reserve one of their bay side cabins. The cabins are in high demand, so
reserve a year in advance. **Loggerhead** and **Sandspur Beach** are on the
ocean side. The protected, **Calusa Beach** is between the bridges.

The trail to the old railroad bridge is a great spot to view sunset. But,
be sure to snap a photo of the railroad bridge. As previously mentioned,
the Flagler Railroad Bridge and the old highway above it – is falling

Old Bahia Honda Railroad Bridge. Scout Key, MM 35

down. Saving it would require a complete rebuild. Notice there is a lower and upper level. Unlike the many other bridges, the lower level where the train operated could not be widened due to its design. So, they put the road on the upper level, another incredible achievement. The concrete pilings are still in great shape for their age. I could imagine a new walkway across them one day. Bahia Honda's dive boat, **Sundance**, offers daily trips to **Looe Key** to snorkel the reef. The concession also rents kayaks on fair weather days.

The south facing ocean side beaches suffered a direct hit from Hurricane Irma. But, like the rest of the Lower Keys, **Bahia Honda State Park** did an amazing job to return to greatness. Opened back up in 2022, same as with the Old Seven Mile Bridge to Pigeon Key, these spots offer a couple of more great options for the visitor and local alike to enjoy.

As you look out to the water in-between the Bahia Honda bridges, you are viewing world class fishing grounds. Tarpon come here in great numbers every April - June, as do enthusiasts from around the globe. Catching a tarpon is akin to roping a bucking bronco, as these 150 LB stallions fight with every last bit of strength. You often hear the holler, *"Yahoo!"* followed by other hoots, as once hooked, tarpon take to the air. The anchor is quick-released and the fight is on. If lucky enough, the angler will bring the fish to the boat after a half hour or so battle. They then snap a photo to cement the memory – and carefully release it.

The Horseshoe swimming hole. Scout Key, MM 35

Just over the Bahia Honda bridge on Scout Key *(named in 2010 for the two adjoining scout camps on it)* is the **Horseshoe** swimming hole at MM 35, bay side. Named for it's U-shaped crane road impression, the area was quarried for material to connect the few islands that now make up Scout Key. Also, to supply on-ramp material to the new highway bridge. The Horseshoe is a great alternative to swim and fish for those without a boat to get out of the heat, or scuba practice. There is good snorkeling along the rocks on the south end. When the wind is up, the Horseshoe is a pretty popular spot for kiteboarding too. It is the best known quarried swimming hole between Bahia Honda and Key West. *Note: wet shoes or flip flops are recommended. Also, the path can be slippery.*

At the foot of the Horseshoe parking lot, there is a boardwalk through the mangroves out to the base of the new bridge. You can walk under the bridge to view of the old Bahia Honda Rail Bridge, aka *"Broken Bridge"*, and explore the ocean side. Or, if driving up the Keys, there is an area to pull over to park on the ocean side. The Bahia Honda overlook is a common stop for many as a last great photo opportunity as you say goodbye to the Lower Keys. What a view! *Note: This area is regularly patrolled for traffic violators – watch your speed, and no u-turns.*

Continuing down the Keys... on the west end of Scout Key is the Spanish Harbor public boat ramp and the restored fishing bridge. This is a great second best for catching snapper and a wide variety of fish.

You are closing in on **Big Pine Key** and MM 33. Big Pine Key is a bicycle friendly island. But, stay on the bike path rather than US 1 whenever

possible – we don't want you to become a statistic. Big Pine Key is a big island, extending 8 miles north and south and 4 miles east and west, but that is not how it got its name. It is one of the few islands with enough earth substrate and fresh water pockets for big pine trees to grow – and grow they do. I often jest that Big Pine Key feels like a friendly witness protection program. But in truth, locals like to remind others whenever the opportunity presents itself, ..."*Nothin' finer than a Piner.*"

Just over the Spanish Harbor bridge, *(first left)* off US 1 at Long Beach Road, is the **Big Pine Key Resort**, previously known as the Big Pine Key Fishing Lodge. There is a nice ocean side nature trail, and some tame Key deer too. The lodge was acquired by **Cove Communities** in 2021. Similar to Bahia Honda State Park, Big Pine Key Resort is often booked a year in advance. Upgrades include full hook-ups, attractive Airstream and tiki trailer units, and other exciting things to come.

Also here, **Keys Boat Tours**, for eco, sunset, snorkel, fishing, and hands-on boating, navigation, and fishing lessons. Keys Boat Tours is a #1 rated tour operator as deemed by TripAdvisor. You don't have to stay at **Big Pine Key Resort** to enjoy time on the water. Just call **Keys Boat Tours** at 305-699-7166 *keysboattours.com* to set up a tour. Captain Brian and Captain Allison can take you to the Gulf side or backcountry, or to the only living barrier reef in the continental United States. It promises

Greetings from

KEYS BOAT TOURS
BIG PINE KEY RESORT, MM 33

to be a highlight of your Keys visit. Also, down the very scenic Long Beach Road, two B&B's: **Barnacle B&B** and **Deer Run B&B**, both very special with oceanfront views and private beaches.

The **Lower Keys Chamber of Commerce** at MM 31 has many events throughout the year: nautical flea market, craft fair, dolphin tournament, music festival, business social, and more. They do a great job helping to promote local businesses while creating a genuine feel of community. Stop in for literature, info, and even – bathroom use if need be.

If you turn right onto Sands Road, *third right after the curve,* go ten or so blocks to end, you will find the **Big Pine Key Community Park** water views, fields, courts, and a refreshing breeze off of Bogie Channel.

FOOD

Food offerings on Big Pine Key are mostly casual but good. There is **Coco's Kitchen**, a mother and daughter operation that has been in the Keys since 1989 *(Winn Dixie Plaza)*. Think Cuban mix sandwich, avocado salad, and good burgers. Newer establishments include **Paradise BSB** bar restaurant at the curve, friendly service, good food. **Island Deli** *(try the meatball sub)*, and **Big Pine Rooster;** breakfast, lunch and dinner.

The longtime established, **Good Food Conspiracy,** is a hippie meets healthy vibe that's been in business for 40 years! You will find down to earth people, gourmet meets organic, a juice bar, homemade soups, and delicious sandwiches made with organic ingredients. It is just past the flea market in a little strip mall on the ocean side of US 1. Another fun visit on Big Pine Key is the **No Name Pub** – if you can find it.

There is **Coconuts** too, the bar, pool hall, and drive-thru liquor store that has been here for decades. One regular summed up Coconuts as... *"A time capsule for misfits who gather on a daily basis."* If you want to get double buzzed at Coconuts, you can get your haircut here too, **Monica's** – weekends.

Shop

The **Big Pine Flea Market**, perpetually in its final year to make room for a Publix supermarket, is just west of the traffic light on the ocean side. It is at peak operation January - March and worthy of a walk through – open Saturday and Sunday 8AM-2PM. The best deals include produce, tools, knickknacks, sunglasses, and **Mini Donuts**.

The newest addition to Big Pine Key *(at the west end on Pine Channel)* is the very beautiful **Big Pine Swimming Hole**, complete with gazebos, bathrooms, observation deck, and parking – kayak rentals too.

The Not So Little About Big Pine Key

Big Pine Key has **Lower Keys Chamber**, **Generations Seafood Market**, **Sea Center**, **Ace Hardware**, **Overseas Lumber**, **Jigs**, and **Napa**. There is **Big Pine Bicycle Center**, **Lower Keys Tackle** for top notch fishing gear, bait, and seminars too. To get it all to you, **The UPS Store,** in the **Winn Dixie Plaza** (supermarket). We have doctors, dentists, physical therapists and massage therapists to thank. I can personally recommend

Dr. Grider DO, Dr. Troxel DDS and **Barrett Chiropractic PA** – very good people to know when the need demands.

A favorite weekend past time for Keys folks is the very competitive sport of yard sale. *"It's 8AM somewhere"* one might say. At the traffic light intersection of US 1 and Key Deer Boulevard, you will find a telephone pole with yard sale announcements. Another good source of information is a local paper issued each Friday, **News Barometer**. For online yard sales, go to Facebook and search for *Key West Yard Sale, Big Pine / Marathon Yard Sale* and *Lower Keys Yard sale* – these Groups are a great way to get word out, or to ask a question.

Let's go back to the BPK traffic light. Veer left to go up **Key Deer Boulevard**. A 35+ year old secret hippie campground, the **LongHair Ranch**, some now affectionately refer to as the *LawnChair Ranch*. It is just $50 per week per tent site. I was offered a cabin for $25 per night *(plus a chore of option)*. It is a very special place with a zen garden commune feel. If you fit in, you can stay. Those meant to find it – will.

The LongHair Ranch. Big Pine Key

There are a couple of nature paths further up Key Deer Boulevard. One is the **Blue Hole**, home to our resident alligators. The other is **Watson Hammock** nature trail. This is Key deer habitat. You will find plenty little deer here, but please don't feed them. It is illegal. There are more alligators in the fire roads too, so keep your dogs on leash.

Key deer, great white heron, living coral

Key Deer Blvd. is approximately five miles in length. It makes a good route to walk, run, or bike. Before you visit these places stop in to the **National Key Deer Refuge Visitor Center**, just east of the US 1 traffic light on Big Pine Key. *Just a reminder, the maximum speed limit on the Overseas Highway at night on Big Pine is 35 mph; 25 mph on the side roads. Be on the lookout for Key deer – they are known to cross the street without looking both ways.*

It is very convenient to have a supermarket on Big Pine Key, one of the more affordable islands in the Keys. Otherwise, it is Marathon and Key West. The **Winn Dixie Plaza** includes the supermarket and liquor store, **Bealls Outlet, Coco's Kitchen, Rose Dell Realty, Keys Electronics, Pizzaworks, Artists In Paradise, The UPS Store, China Garden** *(good wonton soup and fried dumplings)*, **Bagel Island**, a gym, laundromat, the **Big Pine Key Library**, and the **Tax Collector's** office.

Other places of interest on Big Pine are **Grimal Grove**, a tropical fruit tree farm with a very interesting back story; **Octopuses Garden** for most all landscape needs; and the marine science camp, **Seacamp** – 50+ years of educating and going strong. Seacamp is a wonderful marine science camp for visiting students, and local kids and teens alike.

Critters that exist on the island include Key deer, iguana, box turtle, raccoon, woodrat, alligator, a variety of anoles, lizards, geckos and many others, including Key dog. As for birdlife, one might see ibis, egret, heron, osprey, pelican, cormorant, rooster, chicken, peacock, frigatebird, bald eagle, roseate spoonbill and maybe even a flamingo if you're very lucky.

In the water you will find dolphin, manatee, ray, sea turtle, a great variety of shark, including: nurse, lemon, black tip, hammerhead, bonnethead, and bull to name a few. Although the thought of swimming with sharks may unnerve some, the incidents are very few, so fear not. While fishing, you can catch a variety of snapper, grunt, mackerel, jack and grouper. In fact, there is more of a variety of species in the FL Keys than most anywhere. It is not uncommon to catch five or more different species on a single outing. This is owed to the barrier reef and its proximity to the Gulf Stream – making the Keys a fishing mecca.

The fish on the reef are almost too many to list, and beautiful to look at: yellowtail, parrotfish, angelfish, filefish, butterflyfish, damselfish, shark, ray, sergeant major, hogfish, blue tang *(Dory)*, goliath grouper, barracuda, wrasse, and snapper. If you're very lucky, a spotted eagle ray.

No Name Pub. "A nice place if you can find it." The oldest bar on Big Pine Key. 3 miles north of US 1; turn at the traffic light *(bay side)*

NO NAME

It is not all together known why No Name Key has no name but it is a nice place to visit nevertheless. Go north at the light on Big Pine Key, then veer right onto Wilder Road. Go to the stop sign and turn left. As you continue *(around the bend onto Avenue A)* you will happen upon the **No Name Pub**, actually located on Big Pine Key. Just a little further up is the **Old Wooden Bridge Marina & Resort**. Sadly, the entire property took a major hit from Irma, but they are back up and running – more floating homes than cottages. **Big Pine Kayak Adventures** is also there. Please take one of their great kayak tours. They offer a very special tour into a mangrove cave that is certain to be a highlight of your visit. Capt. Bill and his guides can also take you out to the backcountry and guide you on a very interesting paddle around some shallow water islands.

The former old wooden bridge, *now concrete*, takes you to **No Name Key.** You will find some Key deer here too, especially at dusk. Once over the bridge, there a variety of trail-heads off the main road, Watson Blvd, but go on a dry day, otherwise mud city. *Note: the **All Trails** app for your phone shows trails in the area, and will help keep you from getting lost. There is also the **Strava** app – both free and great. It reminds you to bring your phone with you too, which could be useful if you get into trouble. These apps record distance, time and mph.* The 2.1 mile **Paradise Drive** trail takes you back to an old abandoned quarry. This quarried coral material was used for bridge on-ramp and road fill. It was also sold for aquarium, wall, landscape, gravel, and other functional uses.

There are actually many quarries from Bahia Honda to Key West that have become local swimming holes. Other excavated land, marinas, home developments, etc. helped fill the causeway to build the new highway. The No Name Key quarry is no longer in business. It is now privately owned and no trespassing is allowed. *Note: the **All Trails** app is good insider info for trails on all Keys islands.* If you do go for a hike, perhaps you could bring a garbage bag with you and help keep our trails clean.

After your No Name Key crawl, check out the **No Name Pub**. One peek inside is worth a hundred thousand or more in dollar bills, stapled to every square inch of the place. They have a popular T-shirt selection, but a give-away too, *"I am a tourist or a snowbird"*. Best to wear cool shirts from elsewhere, or *"Sorry what I said while docking the boat",* sort of shirt. But, the atmosphere is fun and the food is okay; pizza, fish sandwich, chicken wings, nachos, and the Cuban sandwich are favorites. It's a cool little place with a lot of history.

Lower Keys Restaurants & Bars

The Keys between Key West and Marathon have yet to gain a reputation for high end food mainly because there isn't a lot. **Kiki's Sandbar Bar and Grille** on Little Torch Key has some nice lunch and dinner options worth a try. Take the first right on Little Torch Key, onto Barry Avenue and you are there. Kiki's is one of the few water view restaurants with a beach feel – and they love dogs. There is an upstairs restaurant / bar, and a bar with tables downstairs too. Kiki's serves lunch and dinner daily. The staff is very friendly, the food is good, and the atmosphere is Keys chill. Kiki's is accessible by boat, and offers nightly live music.

On Ramrod Key, MM 27, two longtime establishments include the **Looe Key Tiki Bar** and **Boondocks Grille & Draft House**. If you are up for live music, drinking, and dancing, albeit stuck in time – the **Tiki Bar**. For good food, great week day happy hour apps, live music, sports TV, and a gift shop – **Boondocks**. They are close enough to compare for yourself, but no comparison really. They are both different and good. Also at Boondocks, a new open air farmer's market – open every Saturday 9AM-2PM. **Looe Key Dive Center,** offers daily snorkel trips to Looe Key – weather permitting of course. Just a few doors down from Boondocks and **Cruz Veterinary**, is **Five Brothers Two**. Five Brothers Two is open for breakfast and lunch. It is family owned and currently run by the woman of the family. I jest that they should now call it Five Sisters.

5 Brothers Two, Cuban grocery and restaurant. Ramrod Key – MM 27

5 Brothers Two offers a variety Cuban sandwiches, empanadas, hot meals, and great Cuban coffee. This Cuban cafe has a screened-in patio with tables in the back. Be sure to try their café con leche, or a buchi, pronounced *"boo-chee"*, a shot of Cuban espresso with sugar, guaranteed to get you going. 5 Brothers Two also sells grocery items, and has a fresh fish market too.

Two restaurants to open right after hurricane Irma are **Tonio's Seafood Shack and Tiki Bar** on Summerland Key MM 25 – think Italian American meets seafood favorites under a shaded Tiki with an accompanied live musician, and **South of the Seven** at the Sugarloaf lodge MM 16 – sophisticated Greek / Mediterranean meets casual Keys. Just past Tonio's on the ocean side is **The Galley Grill** – hearty breakfast and lunch with friendly service.

Square Grouper Bar & Grill, located on Cudjoe Key, MM 22½ stands alone in the eyes of TripAdvisor as the best casual meets gourmet restaurant outside of Key West. Expect to wait for a table though – this popular Lower Keys eatery has a great buzz. *Note: Square Grouper is code for "bale of marijuana".* The restaurant is always packed and takes no reservations. They have cornered the market on the former drug running days of yore, and extend their brand into fun T-shirts, e.g., smoked, baked, and fried. Their cocktail lounge and raw bar, **My New Joint**, makes the wait – super mellow. Of course, happy hour here starts at 4:20PM, a reference that is certain to slip by many – also code for consuming cannabis, dating back to 1971. Also, on Cudjoe is **Broil** *"Small Island Steakhouse."* It too is very busy, and does not take reservations.

Sugarloaf Key boasts one of the oldest restaurants in the Lower Keys, **Mangrove Mama's** MM 20 – with live music and a tropical Keysz vibe. The buildings were originally constructed in the early 1900's as a rail stop station and housed agents working for Flagler's Overseas Railroad.

NEWFOUND HARBOR

Newfound Harbor, Big Munson Island

There are many places to get on the water, and Newfound Harbor is one such place. Convenient to the State Road 4A boat ramp on Little Torch Key. Newfound Harbor / ocean side, is home to **Picnic Island** and a couple of other islands sadly decimated by hurricane Irma. Still, Picnic island remains as a locals gathering spot to enjoy a nice sandbar where you can swim and sip at the same time.

A short distance away is **Little Palm Island. Little Palm Island Resort and Spa** is mainly known to the well-to-do, as one might expect with a $5,000+ per night price tag. Formerly Sheriff's Island in the 80's, its early claim to fame is as the location for the film, PT 109. Little Palm Island also took a direct hit from Irma, but the entire resort and spa has come back better than ever. Take their ferry boat, the Truman from Little Torch Key for lunch or dinner – *reservations required.*

Little Palm Island is part of a chain of barrier islands that are only accessible by boat. These islands, sandwiched between Big Pine Key and Little Palm Island, are mostly in their natural and undeveloped state, save for Cook Island with private homes, and another island or two with a private homes. The body of water around and to the north of these islands is **Coupon Bight**, the 5,400 acre southernmost aquatic preserve.

THE REEF

Parrotfish, Looe Key Marine Sanctuary

On the ocean side, **The Florida Reef Tract** is the third largest barrier reef system in the world after the Great Barrier Reef in Australia, and the Mesoamerican Reef that Mexico, Belize, Guatemala and Honduras share. The Florida Reef Tract extends 360 linear miles from St. Lucie Inlet in Martin County, to the Dry Tortugas in the Gulf of Mexico. In the Florida Keys the reef is approximately 4 miles offshore. People are often surprised to learn how shallow the water is in the Keys, and how few beaches there are considering a 113 mile long archipelago. The barrier reef requires shallow water to live. Its barrier make-up prevents waves to build that would otherwise break sea shells and create sand. The natural sand that is here is a combination of calcium rich algae, dead coral, and parrotfish waste. Parrotfish are prolific eaters of coral, or the zooxanthellae algae within coral. It is said that each parrotfish can produce hundreds of pounds of sand per year.

Several dive shops will take you to Looe Key to snorkel or scuba. Just south and 6 miles off of Big Pine Key, this is the premiere snorkel spot in the Lower Keys. Looe Key is a reef within a Sanctuary Preservation Area

(SPA), and is named after HMS Looe, pronounced *"loo"*, which ran aground on the reef and sank in 1744. Pick your day carefully – you want it to be calm and clear. Check the wind, *windfinder.com*. The most affordable way to go is via a head boat. **Looe Key Dive Center** or **Captain Hook's** are good for larger groups and individuals, but, if for 4 to 6 people I recommend you hire a private charter like **Keys Boat Tours**. The captain will guide you on the dive too, and even take photographs during your outing. A second best, when conditions are prohibitive for the reef, is **Newfound Harbor Marine Sanctuary**, a SPA zone patch reef much closer to shore, and only eight or so feet deep.

The Straits of Florida, often misinterpreted as the Atlantic Ocean, is below the continental US mainland, and generally accepted to be the body of water that lies between the Atlantic Ocean and the Gulf of Mexico – and between the FL Keys and Cuba. Its shoreline is US 1. Out a couple of miles at 25' is Hawks Channel. The channel dips to 45' and back up to 25'. At the four-mile mark, at the reef, the depth ranges from 2' to 30'. Beyond the reef, the fall off is far more dramatic.

At five miles it is 90'. Thereafter, it drops approximately 100' per mile. At ten miles it is 500'. The next fives miles varies between 500' and 650'. At 30 miles out, *the wall*, it is 900' deep. Beyond the wall, the drop goes from 1200' to 2000' and deeper pretty quick. Out here, mahi mahi, tuna, sailfish, wahoo, marlin, swordfish and a myriad of pelagic fish can be sought after. The Gulf Stream distance can vary from 6 to 40 miles offshore, and range 10 to 20 miles in width.

Florida Keys
Backcountry
mangrove
islands

THE BEAUTIFUL BACKCOUNTRY OF THE
FLORIDA KEYS

THE BACKCOUNTRY

While the Gulf Stream and its constant 80° surface temperature helps to keep the Keys subtropical, the Gulf side or *"bay side"* is unique unto itself. Just five or so miles north of US 1 is the backcountry; a wide open prairie filled bowl of water. It is the beautiful blue green yonder where flats boats are often the vehicle of choice due to the very shallow or *"skinny"* water. It is in the backcountry where red mangrove islands dot the landscape. You will see many mangrove islands in the Keys. *FYI: The word "Keys" comes from the Spanish word "cayos", slang for "little blisters".* The roots of these mangrove islands provide nursery habitat for much of the marine life. The branches act as roosts for a variety of bird species. Navigation by boat in the backcountry is a learning curve conquered only with experience, and perhaps a banged up prop early on. A navigational aid might be a stick with a traffic cone atop it, or at other times, barely a stick. This is *"gun it and go"* territory. You often have to stay on plane to avoid running aground. It is the main reason that many visitors choose a guide over renting a boat.

BOMB HOLES & LEDGES

While swimming holes are excavated quarries whose material was used as on-ramp and road fill, bomb holes are random spots throughout the backcountry, or bay side, where bombs were literally dropped as munition practice. Dating back to WWII, bomb holes were the product of aerial defense exercises. There are a few well known holes off Big Pine

Key not too far from US1, another near Little Money Key, and several more just east of Friend Key, back on the bay side. And, that's just around the Bahia Honda area. Much of the bay side is 6'-10' in depth. A bomb hole might be 30' in radius and 15'-20' deep. Bomb hole: home to nurse shark, lobster, grouper, snapper and more.

In the channels between the islands, or grass flats, you will come upon white spots that vary in radius, 10' to 20'. These are ledges. Grouper and lobster are known to hide in both bomb holes and ledges. You will actually find many fish here, tropical and otherwise. Ledges act as protection from predators. Grass flats are home to a variety of snapper year round, but mainly mangrove snapper. In winter months, depending on water temperature, you can find speckled trout, mackerel, cobia and jacks.

OFF THE BEATEN TRACK

A nice drive or bike, right about MM 28 is from US 1 to the end of Big Torch Key. After you pass Barry Avenue, and State Road 4A, you come to **Middle Torch Road**. There is a sign for Big Torch Key *(bay side)*. Turn here and keep going – for seven long yet scenic miles. Low lying mangroves and wetlands abound – birdlife, and more recently Key deer too, so drive carefully. This road takes you from Middle Torch Key to Big Torch Key. Make a left turn onto **Dorn Road**, otherwise you hit a dead end on Middle Torch Key. This left turn takes you across a causeway connecting the islands. The culvert area, midway across, is a good place to have a drink and salute the sun as it sets. The end of Big Torch Key is another four miles away and well worth the ride. The next two miles is off-the-grid, solar and cistern only. Enjoy the drive back. In true Keys fashion, there is only one way in, and one way out.

Another good spot to kayak or walk is on Summerland Key. Pass Tonio's Seafood Shack and take a right on Horace Street. Then, right on Northside Dr., and left on Niles Road – to the end. This is your kayak launch, best at high tide. Just know that the current can get very strong here. The *(very slippery)* trail to the right takes you back to a memory for many of us, what use to be a rustic wooden bridge to the distant island – another victim of Irma. The area is great to explore but bad at dusk, as mosquitoes will mightily attack. The more adventurous might attempt a cross to the island, but wear wet shoes, and beware of tides, and current, and snakes. OK, let's just go to Tonio's for same apps and a drink instead.

Summerland Key offers the last real cluster of shops before you get to Key West. Highlights include **Tonio's**, **Galley Grill**, **Murray's Market** *(think deli, sandwiches, and big cut steaks)*, **Summerland Wine & Spirits**, **Ye Olde English Fly Shop** for world famous fly fishing rigs, **Florida Keys Kayaks & Eco Tours**, and various other shops. **Keys Boat Tours** is here too. And, **Aqua Boat Rentals**, next to the Shell station, 305-849-4498 . Summerland Key even has its own private runway, and homes complete with private hangers. It is worth taking a look. On the west end of Summerland Key is a fishing bridge with ample parking.

Look, up in the sky, it's a blimp, it's white, and it's attached to a tether. It is affectionately known as *"Fat Albert"*, a surveillance blimp operated by Homeland Security and based on Cudjoe Key. It is mostly looking for drug running boats, and I imagine - at Cuba. Turn right at

Blimp Road boat ramp, Cudjoe Key – MM 21½

MM 21½ onto **Blimp Road**. It is the same road where the transfer station *(dump)* is – so look for that sign *(bay side)*, and go all the way to the end. There are beautiful mangroves to either side of Blimp Road, and a boat ramp at the end looking smack dab at the backcountry.

This is a good spot for a dip or to launch a kayak or paddleboard. The adventurous kayaker might paddle to **Knockemdown Key** and **Tarpon Belly Key,** and perhaps even camp out overnight. Just remember, Fat Albert is right above scanning your every sun drenched tropical thought.

Cudjoe Sales, on Cudjoe Key, offers a large selection of fishing gear and tackle. **Low Key Fisheries** is here too, in the event that you want to save time and money *and just buy the darn fish*. Newest to Cudjoe Key is the spectacular, **Underwater Photography Gallery**, right next door to **Square Grouper** and definitely worth a visit. The restaurant, **Broil** is just down the road a piece.

Next, is Upper Sugarloaf Key. It gets pretty sparse along the road here, but in a good way – natural splendor. The water turns from green to milky white depending on the wind – calcium and limestone being stirred up from the sea floor. Some places worthy of a mention are the **Sugarloaf Key KOA** campground and RV park, **Lazy Lakes RV Resort**, **Mangrove Mama's,** and the very popular fishing bridge on US 1. This bridge is also a very popular spot to jump off of, if you dare, *(east end)*.

Bridge Fishing, Old Seven Mile Bridge – MM 40

A license to fish on Keys bridges is required, obtained at any tackle shop or *gooutdoorsflorida.com*. Non-residents must pay a fee. Florida residents do not, but a license is still required. One should be familiar with all fishing regulations: identification, size limit, and bag limit as it changes often. If you do fish, do so responsibly, and please use the **Fish Rules** app. To learn how to bridge fish contact, **Ryan:** *fishthebridges.com*.

Those caught taking too small, or too many, can get fined plenty. There is an art to bridge fishing. Check the weekend warriors impressive array of coolers, carts, rod holders, nets, shade tents, seats, and the like.

Before & After Hurricane Irma

Crawl Key - before

After Hurricane Irma

South Bahia Honda Overlook, Scout Key - before

After Hurricane Irma

Yard, Big Pine Key   before

After Hurricane Irma

Old Wooden Bridge Marina, Big Pine Key - before

Marina 1½ years after Hurricane Irma

After the Storm

Sailboat at Smathers Beach, Key West

Boat at Spanish Harbor Ramp, Scout Key

House off foundation, Big Pine Key

Sunk Houseboat, Stock Island

Destroyed House, Big Pine Key

Destroyed House, Big Pine Key

House right after Hurricane Irma

House renovated with new roof and shingles

You will require a guide and a boat, but a tour of the backcountry is a recommended adventure – **Content Keys** in particular. The backcountry is what the Keys is all about: wilderness, wildlife, mangrove islands, and water – lots of water. And, if you go at low tide, you will see long stretches of white sand beach and abundant birdlife. You might choose to head out with **Keys Boat Tours**. They offer a great *Day On The Water* backcountry tour. Anywhere in the backcountry, near or far, is a special time on the water as long as the conditions are right and you have a knowledgeable guide to lead the way. Two other reliable family fun recreational guides include

Hanging out in the backcountry at low tide

Captain Mike of **Lower Keys Adventure Charters**, and Captain Kendall of **Keys to the Keys Adventures**. You can't go wrong with any of the three.

The backcountry is akin to the outback in Australia – go there if possible. It is the great outdoors like no other. One especially good access point is **Sugarloaf Marina**, MM 17. You are immediately taken into another world – through stretches of mangrove mazes. If you have just one opportunity to see the backcountry of the Keys, do it here.

Sugarloaf Marina is a great place to hop on a charter boat, whether to fish the backcountry or enjoy outer islands like Marvin Key and Snipe Key. Upon your return, the tiki bar at the **Sugarloaf Lodge** has a beautiful view and occasional live music. Or, cool down at **South of the Seven** restaurant. The lodge is a great location relative to Key West. *Note: There is a good Farmers Market at the Lodge every Wednesday from 8AM-3PM.*

BIKE / KAYAK/ PICNIC

Another great outing from the **Sugarloaf Lodge** is to take a bike ride. Directly across US 1 from the Sugarloaf Lodge parking lot is Sugarloaf Boulevard. It is a 3 mile long straight-away that is safe for bikes. Use your **Strava** app here too. You can park at the lodge and enjoy this 6 mile round-trip workout. You can also drive 3 mile stretch, park after the turn *beyond the no parking signs*, and then bike **Loop Road**. Enter

Sammy Creek Landing, aka Sammy's Point, Sugarloaf Key

at the turn/corner. Loop Road, as locals refer to it, is a four mile loop. It is said to be intended as a development but never completed. Lucky us! Today you will find a pedestrian only road, swimming holes, and a bridge that locals call the *"jumping bridge"*. The water is said to be 15-20 feet deep, but best to check before you jump. The views here are lovely.

If you continue driving after the turn and signs, it too is scenic. You will see lots of iguana along the road, big ocean side properties and then... a park at a bridge, **Sammy's Point**. This is a great place to launch a kayak. Just know the current here can be very strong. Water current in the Keys can be nominal one minute and extreme the next. Take caution. There is a cool maze of mangroves here too, so best to turn on your **Strava** app or GPS. All this, covered picnic tables, and a great view.

An all-together different jumping experience can be found over at **Skydive Key West** at **Sugarloaf Shores Airport**, next door to the Sugarloaf Lodge. It is a jump with a view like no other. While there, ask about the infamous pre Irma **bat tower**, an ill fated attempt to rid mosquitoes. Mosquito Control is big business in the Keys and it continually evolves.

As you continue your journey past Sugarloaf Key toward Key West you will soon come to the **Saddlebunch Keys**.

This beautiful scenery through Saddlebunch Keys, MM 12-14, is an **Audubon Sanctuary** habitat. It is a good area to marvel at the ever changing colors of the water. On your way, stop in at **Baby's Coffee**, MM 15 for a cup of joe, or **Baypoint Market** for sandwich, and stretch your legs, and your dogs too, at **Bay Point Park**.

GEIGER KEY

Turn left at MM 10 *(Shell Station)* on **Boca Chica Road** to the end and check out the beach. The far west end has a nude beach. On the way there is a very cool sculptured tree hut. The chain linked fence on the right is the **Naval Air Station**. The **Blue Angels** perform here every few years. If you've never seen them in action – do.

Heading back toward US 1, turn right at the bend onto Geiger Road and to the **Geiger Key Marina & Fish Camp**. Geiger Key restaurant is a great spot for a drink and a meal anytime, especially the fish sandwich, tacos, burger and chicken wings. Their happy hour is very affordable, *weekdays only*. Weekends are great too, often with live music. Sunday afternoon is their BBQ special. The setting: mangroves, water, dogs, friendly people, and a sunset view – super special.

Geiger Key Marina & Fish Camp, Geiger Key MM 10

A boat tour business based out of Geiger Key Marina, **Key West Eco Tours**, has a great deal on kayak and paddleboard rentals. They offer shuttle service to and from Key West. Take a guided tour and paddle through some wonderful mangroves. Best always to go against the wind upon your departure, so to return with the wind at your back. They also offer sail and motor boat tours based out of Key West. Just beyond the park / restaurant is a boat ramp to launch boats, kayaks and paddleboards. It is also a good spot to take a dip for person and dog alike.

THANK YOU

Even though I make mention of several happy hour spots throughout the book, please do your responsible best to *NOT* drink and drive. Also, watch out for other drivers and *texters*. That in mind, I would like to take this opportunity to thank all those who come to our rescue to save lives of locals and visitors alike: police, sheriff, trooper, FWC, USCG, dispatch, fire company, EMT, evacuation transport, hospital, doctors, nurses, etc. Rescue is a big part of life along the Overseas Highway. We don't like the sound of the siren, but we are very grateful that you come to our rescue. *Note: Locals should remember to affix your Trauma Star stickers onto you driver's license for free medevac helicopter transport. And, get your re-entry sticker too.* And, special thanks to all the marine and wildlife rescue people out there who play a very important role taking care of our turtles, dolphins, birds and key deer: wildlife rescue, volunteers, veterinarians, etc.

STOCK ISLAND

OK, let's head west, but, first you might want to check out **100 Miles to Cuba**, MM 10 *(bay side)* if only for their flan and Cuban coffee. They have an all day breakfast burrito too. This local spot is worthy of a stop. Another Keysz vibe restaurant just a tad west is **Bobalu's Southern Café** – think comfort food, pizza and beer.

Next up: Stock Island. If you enjoy lap swimming as I do, there is a nice outdoor pool at

College of the Florida Keys pool, Stock Island

The College of the Florida Keys. Turn right onto College Road just before MM 5 – at the **H** *(hospital)* sign. The pool is behind the school. There is a $5 fee per person to swim. For internet access, the college library offers free WiFi and a great view of the Gulf. Also, the college is home the **Tennessee Williams Theatre**. The **Key West Golf Club**, a public 18 hole course is just across the street *(rental clubs available)*, as is the hospital. Continue on College Road and it will take you to the **Florida Keys SPCA**, the **Key West Tropical Forest & Botanical Garden**, and back to US 1.

EXPLORE

Stock Island has several eateries worth checking out: **Roostica** *(wood fired pizza)*, **Hogfish Bar & Grill** *(classic dockside seafood)*, and **Croissants de France** *(breakfast / lunch)*. If coming from Key West, veer right onto McDonald Avenue and go a few blocks to 3RD Street for **Roostica**. To find **Hogfish Bar & Grill** continue one block to at 4TH Avenue *(West Marine)*, turn right, and take the first left onto Front Street. If Cuban is your desired fare, try **El Siboney** on 4TH Avenue between Front Street and Shrimp Road. The **Hogfish Bar & Grill** and ⌐⌐⌐ **Harbour Marina** is quintessential Keys and a great discovery: good

Hogfish Bar & Grill at Safe Harbour Marina, Stock Island

food and friendly service – along side houseboats, carpenter shops, an art gallery, and the **Lost Kitchen Supper Club** event space. It'll make you want to move here. Try the hogfish sliders or fingers. The chowders are delicious too. Enjoy a meal dockside and take a stroll afterwards. For the gourmet foodie, continue up Front Street, past the shrimp boats and try **The Docks Restaurant + Raw Bar**.

Stock Island has the feel of old Key West. Though named for its herds of livestock back in the day, Stock Island is more sea-to-table than farm-to-table. It has some of the last working boatyards for shrimpers, lobstermen, and commercial fishermen. **Fishbusterz**, the largest wholesale fishery and seafood market in Florida, delivers fresh seafood to most every restaurant in the Keys. That aside, most anything nautical can be made on Stock Island, fabrication heaven meets swanky marinas.

Stock Island Yacht Club & Marina, Oceans Edge Resort, and **Stock Island Marina Village** have paved the way from old Stock Island quite handsomely. **The Perry Hotel** at **Stock Island Marina Village** is very impressive both in design and execution, modern yet rustic with a restaurant, **Matt's Stock Island Kitchen and Bar**, and two other dockside bars, **Salty Oyster** and **Sloppy Joes Dockside**. They also boast a pool, marina, and water views. **Matt's** has an excellent grilled octopus appetizer. **Oceans Edge Resort & Marina** has beautiful ocean views and pools galore. The restaurant,

Yellowfin Bar & Grill is worth a taste. Both hotels have regular shuttle services to Old Town, Key West. The Perry and Oceans Edge offer a lovely respite to hotels in Old Town, and can be more affordable too.

Other places of interest on Stock Island include **Boyd's Campground, Robbie's Marina, Stockyard Studios, We Cycle** *(bike shop and rentals)*, **Hurricane Hole** *(dockside bar, grill, marina)*, and **Lazy Dog Adventures** *(kayak and paddleboard rentals and tours)*.

Go Fish

Fishing the bridges, Bahia Honda Bridge

People who visit the Florida Keys cover the spectrum: people who like to drink, eat, and fish. And, those who wish to get fit, tanned, and rejuvenated. As for locals, there are people who get on the water every single day, and others who have not been on a boat in years.

When winter comes, snowbirds, and tourists double the population. The big draw to the Keys for many is fishing. Fishing for snapper, porgy, and jacks is very popular – by bridge or boat. Come April, migrating tarpon arrive in impressive numbers, as do anglers from around the globe. Tarpon, along with permit, and bonefish is the stuff bucket lists are made of. Grouper season opens May 1. Big mutton and mangrove snapper are biting too. As are dolphinfish (mahi) and blackfin tuna. It is a fishing paradise for many. Then, comes summertime, when the snowbirds migrate back north and the school year ends. Floridians from

Lobster Mini Season is an annual, 2 day period the last Wed and Thurs of July.

the mainland make their annual pilgrimage to the Keys, including many Miami based Cuban families who come here to boat and fish.

Summertime is the right time for fishing, but challenging too. Due to the heat, many prefer to fish deeper and later – or very early, e.g., commercial yellowtail fishermen push off the dock by 5AM, and are back by 11AM. Night fishing delivers big time, but pitch dark and boating is a whole other learning curve. You can't go wrong at a patch reef for mangrove snapper. And, if yellowtail fishing, you might find some nice mutton snapper, or even big kingfish below. When in doubt – chum!

Lobster mini season in late July, brings some 30,000 visitors – many of whom make it an annual tradition. It is always a bit crazy and dangerous, due to too many people and accidents. Many locals would like to see mini season come to an end. One surprising thing about Keys boating, aside from mini season, is that you can go miles into the backcountry and not see another boat. You can literally have the entire sea and sky to yourself – year round. On the ocean side too, there is ample room for everyone. Some boaters might come close to you, but it is likely because they are not catching, and curious to see if you are. I didn't say fishing was necessarily easy – it is not, but it is very popular. For many, it is simply the challenge of trying to become a good angler that keeps them here. And, it might take a while. Yet, another excuse to stay. My other new book, **Boat Fish Live** *(boatfishlive.net)* offers lessons in motor boating, sailing, and fishing. If you could use a catching lesson, or any other, contact Capt. Brian at Keys Boat Tours 305-699-7166.

Conch Republic

Visitors to the Keys today will likely take notice of the **Conch Republic** flag, bumper sticker, T-shirt, and license plate – sold everywhere. Some are familiar with the term **Conch**, pronounced *"konk"*, others are not. For many, it is the mollusk shell that you hold to your ear to listen to the ocean. For others, it is the conch fritter that comes to mind, the delicious appetizer made with meat from within the shell. That said, similar to turtle, conch is no longer legal to harvest in the Keys. It is still plentiful in the Bahamas, the place from which the Keys imports it. Many early settlers of Key West are descendants of Bahamian immigrants who have raised families here. As such, the term **Conch** was originally coined as one who is born and raised in Key West. Today, even the local high school sports teams proudly carry the name, **Key West Conchs**. Transplants feel a sense of belonging too. One can become a **Fresh Water Conch**, no matter where they were born, if one lives in Key West (or the Lower Keys) year round for seven consecutive years.

The term **Conch Republic** is a separate matter altogether. It was born out of protest in 1982 when the US Customs and Border Patrol erected a check point in hopes to discourage illegal immigrants and drugs. As one can imagine, the check point was very unpopular to Keys visitors.

"WE SECEDED W

Key West City Council, and then Mayor, Dennis Wardlow ⌐
the checkpoint was hurting tourism and hindering traffic. H
cil insisted that the check point come down. When their co
deaf ears, and their court battle lost, the Mayor and City c
that since the citizens of the Keys are being treated like a foreign country,
complete with a border and guard patrol, that Key West should perhaps
secede from the United States, and become a foreign nation. It would be
called the **Conch Republic**. The threat was followed with a request of one
billion dollars in foreign aid.

What was both serious and tongue-in-cheek, turned out to be a market-
ing boon for tourism in the Keys. The check point was soon lifted and the
Conch Republic would forever be cemented in Keys folklore. April 23 is
Independence Day in Key West a.k.a., the **Conch Republic**. It is celebrated
each year with an entire week and a half of festivities on both land and sea,
complete with a parade.

The **Bloody Battle** is a highlight of the celebration. This good-spirited battle
pits the Conch Republic Navy against the reviled federal forces, with weap-
ons ranging from water cannons, to sponges, flying Cuban bread, and toilet
paper. Spectators are invited to view the debacle from Bloody Battle Parties
at the **Sunset Pier** at **Ocean Key Resort**, and the **Sunset Deck** and **Bistro
245** at the **Westin Resort & Marina**.

Following the battle, a victory party is scheduled at the **Schooner Wharf Bar**
to commemorate the Conch Republic Navy's triumph over the evil forces of
the *"United States Border Patrol"*. Party goers will definitely have something
to celebrate, since the Republic's naval forces never lose. The festival's oldest and most famous event is the annual **Conch Republic Red Ribbon Bed
Race**. Colorfully decorated wheeled beds are propelled down Duval Street
by drag queens during this daytime slumber party gone wild. *"Bedlam"* is
virtually guaranteed. The race raises money for Key West's **AIDS Help, Inc.**

The **Conch Republic** and the Keys laid back lifestyle are a mirrored reminder that there is the mainland US, and then there is the Keys, unique and
independent, with a flag all its own – to fly high and proud.

...ny place where you can cover your overhead, make a decent living, continuously learn, be creative, and get healthy – is a good place to be. You might already live there. For some, it is the Keys and fishing. For others, it is to turn a leaf and start anew. For more than a handful, it was just a dream. They came, they tried, and they had to leave. It is beautiful here, but it is not easy when you compare overhead to income. Rent, food, and fuel are more expensive here than on the mainland. Good jobs, the ones that pay a better salary, are easier to come by nowadays. But housing, especially since the hurricane, and Covid, is out of reach for many. Lots of people who visit the Keys often want the eternal vacation. They want to eat, drink, and fish, and do it again the next day – five days off and two days on. This is affectionately known as Keys Disease. So, be warned, but not now. Now, we are conched out, loving life!

KEY WEST

Key West, Florida's southernmost point, lies roughly 90 miles north of Cuba. Famed for its timber framed, tin roofed conch houses, and roaming chickens and roosters, Key West is chock-full of history from Bahamian wreckers, commercial fishermen, spongers, and Cuban cigar makers, to the shadier rum runners and drug smugglers of olde. Key West has been home to many authors including Ernest Hemingway, Tennessee Williams, Truman Capote, Elizabeth Bishop, and Robert Frost. A good way to learn some of the history and see the sites is to

Welcome to Key West Sign

Since 1958 the Conch Train is one of Florida's and Key West's most popular attractions

Conch Train
KEY WEST

ride the conch train or one of the tour trollies, then go back the attractions that appeal to you later on. The Hemingway Home is by far one of the most popular attractions in Key West save for its iconic watering holes on Duval Street, and the Southernmost Point Buoy – a must photo op for many.

When you arrive to Key West you have an immediate decision to make; should I turn left – or right? If during the day, left *(South Roosevelt Blvd.)* takes you toward open ocean views, hotels, and eventually – **Smathers Beach**. The **Key West International Airport** is here too.

Smathers Beach, Key West MM1

here, **Fort East Martello Museum**. It the residence of the infamous ˌted doll, **Robert**. Remember to ask for his permission prior to taking a photo – or hex. See *robertthedoll.org*.

Right on North Roosevelt Blvd. takes you to malls, and the option to visit either side of Old Town, straight via Truman Avenue for the ocean side, or right over the Palm Avenue Bridge to the Old Town docks.

Should you decide to go left, Smathers Beach is a fun place to people watch, enjoy shrimp boats at sea, and on windy days – kiteboarders in action. If the mood strikes to *"Say Yes"* in the southernmost way, you can do so on Smathers Beach. **Say Yes In Key West**, *sayyesinkeywest.com* does a very nice job for simple yet beautiful beach nuptials, or choose from one of their exceptional Key West venues.

White Street Pier, aka Ed Knight Pier, Key West

Pass Smathers Beach, go around the bend and make your first left. Go to the stop sign, **White Street**, and park for free at the bocci ball courts and **Key West Wildlife Center**. Take a walk out to **White Street Pier** and the **Key West AIDS Memorial**.

I urge you to go inside the fort building adjacent to Higgs Beach. It is the friendlier **West Martello Tower**, home to the **Key West Garden Club**, just a $1 or $2 donation will do. It is very serene and beautiful inside. Next to the tower on the east side is an **African Burial Ground**, believed to be America's only African refugee cemetery. To the west is Higgs Beach, and the very captivating restaurant, **Salute!**

Hemingway Home, Key West

NAVIGATION

If you come to Key West at night with a destination of **Old Town** in mind, turn left at the light, and go three blocks to another light, Flagler Avenue. Turn right on Flagler and go *(30 mph)* two miles to White Street. Go right on White Street, across the island, to Southard Street. Turn left on Southard and go all the way to the Truman Annex entrance, Thomas Street, two blocks below Duval Street, and turn right. If after 6PM, park for free behind the Courthouse. This area is convenient to the **Green Parrot Bar**, **Blue Heaven**, **Santiago's Bodega**, **Truman Annex**, **Fort Zachary Taylor State Park**, **Hemingway Home**, **Garbo's Grill** (food truck), and **Duval Street**.

For sunset at **Mallory Square** *(sunset celebrated each evening complete with vendors, carnival performers and animal acts)* and the **Key West Bight** *(historic seaport walk and restaurants)*: drive up Fleming, *(one block over)* to Simonton Street. Go left on Simonton to Caroline Street, turn right on Caroline to the municipal lot.

Old Town is where you want to concentrate. Just know that this is the widest part of the island, so best not to walk it all. But, do bring comfortable foot wear. If visiting by day, I highly recommend sunscreen, and a hat. A great way to explore Key West on your own, is to rent a bicycle. You are more free to go where you want, and you'll feel like a local. **We Cycle** *(Southard St)*, or **Eaton Bikes** *(Eaton Street)* will get you

.olling. Have ID with you, obey traffic rules, and watch for pedestrians and cars. Another great way to save your feet is to take advantage of the free Duval Loop bus. Whatever you do, do not drink and drive.

MY KEY WEST TO DO LIST

The *"To Do"* list for Key West promises to entertain, inspire and inform. It includes beach, pool, sightseeing, food trucks, drinking, tours, and then some – even a drag show if you're game. All that, and quiet time too. It is enough to keep you busy for an entire day (or days). But, it can be exhausting too. Make a plan and stick to it. Then, see how you feel and improvise. Many people try to spend four hours on the water in the Lower Keys, then go down to Key West for the late afternoon and evening. Then, make the hour drive back. It is too much people. If you can spend a night or two in Key West instead, do so.

Blue Heaven, Corner of Thomas & Petronia Streets, Key West

FOOD

It's hard to recommend a best place in Key West for a great meal. Several restaurants achieve this *"best"* status often. That said, a best dinner spot from a recent experience of mine is **Blue Heaven**, amazing scallop appetizer and snowy grouper entree. Then, there's **Santiago's Bodega**, incredible tapas, wine, dessert and atmosphere. I also like **Little Pearl** ⁻ish **House & Wine Bar**. On any given night, these and several other who strive to create a special dining experience – might be the best.

Key West To Do List:

- The College of the Florida Keys *(pool, library)*
- The Botanical Garden
- Hogfish Bar / Safe Harbour Marina *(meal and stroll)*
- Smathers Beach
- White Street Pier
- Higgs Beach
- West Martello Tower *(great garden)*
- Southernmost Point
- Key West Churches
- Hotel lobbies and grounds
- Santiago's Bodega *(tapas)*
- Blue Heaven *(scallop appetizer, key lime pie)*
- Little Pearl *(fish house & wine bar)*
- Key West Bait & Tackle *(cool bar)*
- Green Parrot Bar *(sound checks – weekends)*
- Key West Butterfly and Nature Conservatory
- Florida Keys Eco-Discovery Center *(free)*
- Fort Zachary Taylor State Park *(beach, sunset, fort)*
- Conch Train *(Old Town tour)*
- Hemingway Home *(and the six toed cats)*
- Mel Fisher Museum *(shipwreck treasure)*
- Key West Cemetery *(stroll)*
- Mallory Square *(a fun sunset – if only once)*
- San Carlos Institute
- La Te Da *(drinks, dinner, drag show)*
- 5 Brothers *(Cuban coffee, great sandwiches)*
- El Siboney *(Cuban food)*
- Sunset Sail *(Hindu, Argo Navis, When and If)*
- Jet ski ride around Key West

See the map on page 73 for points of interest.

ides **Louie's Backyard, Seven Fish, The Flaming Buoy Filet** Da, **A&B Lobster House, Café Marquesa, Prime Steak**elle, **Hot Tin Roof, Kaya Island Eats** and last but not least, naid. These are higher end places.

For casual fare, too many to list, but I like **Onlywood Grill** on Caroline St., wood fired pizza and more. **Pepe's**, the oldest restaurant in Old Town is famous for a reliable breakfast, rustic outdoor setting and a tasty Bloody Mary. Just a few doors away, **Harpoon Harry's**, also

Pepe's on Caroline Street, Key West

has a good breakfast, lunch, pie, and coffee *(counter and tables)*. And, a nightly $12.⁹⁵ blue plate special. Another popular place is **Caroline's Cafe** *(310 Duval)* – for affordable, tasty, and good portions. **5 Brothers**, Southard Street, is a hidden gem and local's hot spot. **Goldman's Deli**, a local's breakfast and bagel spot with a NY feel is in the Overseas Market *(mall)* off US 1 near Home Depot. **B.O.'s Fish Wagon** has a great, if not messiest hamburger and fries. **The Cafe**, vegetarian and seafood off Duval is well worth a visit. The food truck, **Garbo's Grill** at **Hank's Saloon** has great tacos and burritos. **Cuban Coffee Queen** is another popular alternative, but no seating. I like their slogan, *"Do Stupid Things Faster"*. **El Siboney** has some wonderful and affordable Cuban food and flan. If Irish food and a perfectly poured pint is calling your palate, **Shanna Key Irish Pub & Grill**. **Thai Island** for sushi and curry. And, try the Caribbean fare at **Pepper Pot Island Cafe**, 730 Emma Street.

The Bull & Whistle Bar, 224 Duval Street. With the clothing optional rooftop bar, Garden of Eden

DRINK

There is no shortage of bars to crawl near Duval: **Captain Tony's Saloon**, **Green Parrot bar**, **Hogs Breath Saloon**, **Smokin' Tuna Saloon**, **Irish Kevin's**, **Cowboy Bill's**, **Rick's Bar**, and last but not least, **Sloppy Joe's**. On the ocean side of Old Town: **The Salty Angler**, **La Te Da**, **Southernmost Beach Cafe** / bar, and the **Bottle Cap** are favorites.

The **Half Shell Raw Bar**, **Boathouse Bar & Grill**, **Alonzo's Oyster Bar**, **Two Friends Patio**, and **Onlywood Grill** – have good happy hour specials. If between 7AM and 7PM, visit **Key West Bait & Tackle**. Anchor up beside an affable angler sipping suds at the **Live Bait Lounge**. It is a great little Key West hide-away with an impressive and affordable beer selection. Oh, and they have tackle too.

Another notable place is the **Bull & Whistle Bar**. The **Bull** is the oldest open air bar in Key West, always with live entertainment. The **Whistle** is the upstairs bar with an elevated view of Duval Street. The roof top bar, the **Garden of Eden**, is the only clothing optional bar in Key West. Hanging out at the Garden takes on a whole new meaning. Feel free!

MUSIC

Jimmy Buffet was of course the biggest musical star to come out of Key West. Today, many musicians, some seasoned / some new call the Keys home. Current troubadours to look out for include **Wyatt Hurts and the Painkillers**, **Robert Douglas**, **Brian Roberts**, **Happy Dog**, **The Red Elvises**, and **Howard Livingston** to name a few. These and other

Green Parrot Bar, corner of Southard and Whitehead, Key West

talented musicians perform regularly throughout the Lower Keys. Music venues include **The Key West Theater**, **San Carlos Institute**, **Red Barn Theater**, **The Key West Amphitheater**, **Green Parrot Bar,** and many other bars and restaurants. **The Studios Of Key West**: artist space for artists, writers, and musicians, also host special performances on occasion, *tskw.org*.

The **Green Parrot Bar** is mecca for many with or without music. *"Sound Checks"* 5:30PM - 7PM every Friday and Saturday, are always a lot of fun – great music performed by local and traveling bands alike, including blues, funk, rock, zydeco, and then some. All that, and Jazz Sundays 1PM - 4:30PM You can find it exactly one block south of the

MM 0 sign on Whitehead and Southard Streets. Key West special place. There is music in the air, special architecture to happy locals and visitors, and remarkable banyan, kapok, and fi appreciate. Be sure to take a photo at MM 0.

At the bottom of Southard Street is **Truman Annex**. The guard house gives a look of private neighborhood but it is public space – walk, bike, or drive in freely. The Annex is a welcome retreat from Old Town. It is also another parking option for the area. The revitalized **Truman Waterfront Park** opened in 2018 with amphitheater, splash and play area, and lots of green space. The **Florida Keys Eco-Discovery Center** is here too – free of charge, and very worthwhile. Further inside is **Fort Zachary Taylor**, an 87 acre state park with a pre-Civil War Fort, **Fort Taylor.** The park has a great beach *(rocky though, remember those wet shoes)*, abundant shade, picnic tables, and good snorkeling. It has hiking and biking trails too, Drive in for a nominal fee, park all day, and enjoy a lovely sunset experience with quiet water views – *a good alternative to Mallory Square.* The north end of the annex you will find **The Little White House**, originally built for Navy officer's in 1890, it was the winter White House for President Harry S Truman.

CHURCHES

Among the many beautiful churches in Old Town, **Saint Mary Star of the Sea** on Truman is the oldest Catholic church in South Florida, and named as Minor Basilica by the Vatican in 2012. Another beauty is the 100 year old **Saint Paul's Episcopal Church** on Duval Street. And, in Bahama Village, the **Cornish Memorial AME Zion Church** is the oldest African American church in Key West, on Whitehead Street.

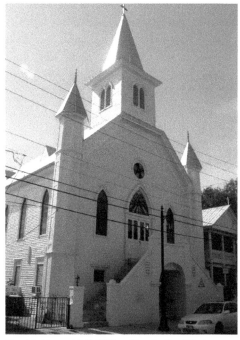

Cornish Memorial AME Zion Church, Key West

I love Key West, but one can only take so much of Duval Street. If you feel the need to rest your feet, make yourself welcome to any place of worship, or perhaps in the lobby / lounge of most any hotel. It's fun to check out different hotels on occasion, even just to tour the grounds or to enjoy a drink at a beach side bar as a getaway from the norm.

The **Southernmost House**, on the ocean side of Duval has lovely grounds, pool, and **Seaside Cafe**. Open to public 11:30AM to 8PM. Try the lobster pizza. At **La Concha** hotel, Key West's tallest building, you can get a coffee at Starbucks and enjoy a comfortable chair inside the lounge. You might instead prefer an afternoon glass of wine at the hotel's, **Wine-O** bar. It is a wonderful respite from people overload and pavement pounding. Your feet will thank me – your sunburn might too.

Pier House Resort & Spa is a cool place to take a peek inside. They have a lovely restaurant, pool, beach and the legendary **Chart Room** Cocktail Lounge, affectionately said to be a dive bar with a resort built around it. The **Hyatt Centric Key West Resort & Spa** has a great display of live rescued turtles *(beyond the lobby)*. There are perhaps as many as 50 fresh water variety, and several different species. And, last but not least, there is **Casa Marina**, conceived by railroad tycoon Henry Flagler – complete with beach, bar, pool, and view. You don't have to stay at a hotel to enjoy it, but non guests are limited to restaurant and tiki bar use only.

The Southernmost House, Key West

Simonton Beach and Lagerheads Beach Bar, Key West

Lagerheads Beach Bar at the Gulf side of Simonton Street offers food and drink selections, beach chairs, lounges, umbrellas, and a bathroom too. This is a sweet little beach for a quick dip, but **FYI:** do not dive off of the pier. It is very shallow and you could suffer severe injuries. Lagerheads also offers live music, and super affordable boat tour options on **Rum Runner.** You can purchase one seat, or rent the entire boat for a six person private tour. **Note:** if so desired, this is a BYOB vessel.

If your feet feel fine, and can still take some pounding, there are several different walking tours to be had: **Original Key West Pub Crawl, Seafood Lover's Tasting & Cultural Walking Tour,** and **The Dark Side of Key West Ghost Tour** to name a few. For those of you who tackled Key West wearing the wrong foot wear, the hotel lobby crawl might be the perfect option for you.

Hyatt Centric Fresh Water Turtle Sanctuary

Go Sailing

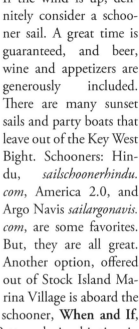

If the wind is up, definitely consider a schooner sail. A great time is guaranteed, and beer, wine and appetizers are generously included. There are many sunset sails and party boats that leave out of the Key West Bight. Schooners: Hindu, *sailschoonerhindu.com*, America 2.0, and Argo Navis *sailargonavis.com*, are some favorites. But, they are all great. Another option, offered out of Stock Island Marina Village is aboard the schooner, **When and If**,

When and If, built for George Patton in 1939

sailwhenandif.com, built for General George Patton, during his time in WW II. *"When the war is over, and if I live through it, Bea and I are going to sail her around the world,"* the general was quoted as saying.

An altogether different option, if you wish to take the helm yourself, **Key West Community Sailing Center**, near Garrison Bight is one of the best kept secrets in Key West – just $190 per year!

Stay

As for where to stay, google *"Best hotel deal in Key West"*. Old Town gets all the glory, and for good reason, but good deals for hotels and food are few and far between anymore. Supply and demand has noticeably taken over. That said, on North Roosevelt Blvd, try **Key West Marriott Beachside Hotel**. Don't worry about being too far from the action, they have a shuttle that goes to Old Town on a regular basis. And, they have a nice restaurant too, **Town & Tavern**. **24 North** and **The Gates** hotel might be a bit more affordable. A little further down is **Havana Cabana**. Come morning time, on the top of the island, walk or jog the ocean side **Overseas Heritage Trail**, yet another great walk and bike spot.

Casa Marina, a luxury hotel built by Henry Flagler to accommodate the passengers arriving on his Overseas Railway.

Some lovely, if not pricey boutique hotels in Old Town include **Eden House, Heron House, The Gardens Hotel**, and **Orchid Key Inn**. You can enjoy live music at The Gardens Hotel every evening from 5PM to 7PM. And, jazz most Sundays.

If money is not an issue, front and center Old Town resorts include **Hyatt Centric Key West Resort & Spa, Pier House Resort & Spa**, and **The Galleon Resort and Marina** – each with a pool and small beach. **Casa Marina** and other ocean side resorts offer a welcome break from Old Town, surrounded by a lovely neighborhood, and at the same time, only minutes away from the action. For those of you on a tight budget, you might want to consider an **Airbnb**, even if on a boat. Another option, the **Seashell Motel and Key West Hostel** – has private rooms and dorms. There are ten beds in the dorm / hostel, approximately $99 per bed, versus $549+ tax for hotel bed in high season, but prices vary. It too is in the heart of Old Town – so something for everyone.

For a tropical getaway there is **Sunset Key Cottages**, a secluded island resort just off of Key West. Rent a cottage or just come fore a special meal at the award-winning **Latitudes** restaurant – one of the best restaurants in the Florida Keys – *advance reservations required.*

THE IDEAL VISIT

Your visit to the Lower Keys might be the eat too much, drink too much, spend too much option. Or, it could be the get fit, tanned and

The End of the Rainbow Sign, Key West – MM 0

rested approach. Either way, there is plenty to do and enjoy. Mix it up with exercise, sightseeing and dining out, as long as you have the best possible trip that you came here for – memorable, relaxing, and fun.

To maximize your Keys visit for ultimate pleasure, I recommend that you mix up your visit with a couple of nights stay in Key West, and a couple of nights at another Lower Keys establishment like **Sugarloaf Lodge**, **Parmer's Resort**, an **Airbnb**, or the high end **VRBO, Sterling Bay House**. It has water views, a boat dock, and pool. It is ideal for wedding parties too, *www.vrbo.com/2565281*. Or call direct, 305-360-2915.

The following itinerary will make your vacation to the Keys complete, **Marathon: Turtle Hospital, Dolphin Research Center, Aquarium Encounters, Pigeon Key, Sombrero Beach**, kayak tour, and restaurants, **Castaways**, etc. **Lower Keys:** Take a private snorkel or fishing charter with **Keys Boat Tours**. See Key deer, explore roads by car, take a hike or two, go to a few restaurants – and then, **Key West: Hemingway Home,** a Sunset schooner sail, a nice dinner at **A&B Lobster House, Blue Heaven, Santiago's Bodega, Nine One Five, Seven Fish, Little Pearl** – *or all.* Perhaps a cocktail off Duval afterward, and cap it off at **Aqua Bar & Nightclub** or **La Te Da** for a fun and lively drag show.

If you have an extra day, I recommend a trip out to **Dry Tortugas National Park**, 70 miles west of Key West, in calm conditions whenever ⁚ble. A very special visit is to camp out there for a night or three. ˙ speed catamaran **Yankee Freedom III**, boards at 7:30AM from

70 Miles west of Key West is the Dry Tortugas National Park. 100 square mile park is mostly open water with seven small islands.

GREETINGS FROM THE DRY TORTUGAS

the Key West ferry terminal, returning at 5:30PM. If camping, you can resupply ice and water when the boat arrives the next day. You can also purchase lunch on the boat. Or, go via sea plane, *keywestseaplanecharters.com* for half or full day options. But, book these well in advance as they are often sold out.

You can now say that you have seen the Lower Keys like a local. You discovered places that can otherwise take years and years to learn about. You did a lot but there is still a lot more to do. And, so you've already planned your return trip. Or, like many, you started looking into real estate options. It is not uncommon.

The fortunate get to fly out of **Key West International Airport**, perhaps even direct to your home state airport. Or, luckier still – you decided to stay. You won't be the first. But, your desire to return to the Lower Keys is all that this little guide book hopes to achieve. That, and to help you get some good photos of your trip. See the complete photo list on the following page – *Say Keys!*

Thanks for visiting the Lower Keys. Please tell friends and family about us, and please come back. You can gift this book to a friend, or better yet, buy them a copy and keep this one as a memento. In the meantime, keep us on the tip of your tongue with our delicious key lime pie recipe, page 74. It has been a pleasure to be your guide.

Recommended photos and selfies: Say Keys!

- ❏ This is you at the Seven Mile Bridge
- ❏ This is you at Veteran's Beach
- ❏ This is you on a paddleboard in a mangrove cave
- ❏ This is you posing with your convertible rental car
- ❏ This is you at the No Name Pub
- ❏ This is you on a bike ride up Key Deer Blvd.
- ❏ This is you photographing Key deer
- ❏ This is you fishing with Capt. Brian and Keys Boat Tours
- ❏ This is you at the Big Pine Key Flea Market
- ❏ This is you at the Horseshoe swimming hole
- ❏ This is you in a backcountry lagoon *(if you're lucky enough)*
- ❏ This is you at Sammy's Point *(Sugarloaf Key)*
- ❏ This is you at Geiger Key Marina
- ❏ This is you at Oceans Edge Resort sipping a Bloody Mary
- ❏ This is you at the White Street Pier
- ❏ This is you at 5 Brothers *(Cuban mix, and cafe con leché)*
- ❏ This is you at the Green Parrot Bar
- ❏ This is you at the Southernmost Point
- ❏ This is you and a Key West Rooster
- ❏ This is you on the Conch Train
- ❏ This is you and a Piña Colada at South Beach, Key West
- ❏ This is you at Blue Heaven restaurant
- ❏ This is you at the Hogfish Bar / Safe Harbour Marina
- ❏ This is you posing in front of a shrimp boat
- ❏ This is you at Mallory Square *(sunset)*
- ❏ This is you at Pepe's *(breakfast)* Caroline Street
- ❏ This is you at B.O.'s Fish Wagon across the street
- ❏ This is you at the helm of a schooner
- ❏ This is you and a Kapok tree *(KW Courthouse)*
- ❏ This is you at Fort Zachary Taylor State Park
- ❏ This is you in with Robert the doll *(Ask permission!)*
- ❏ This is you at Simonton Beach / Lagerhead's Beach Bar
- ❏ This is you at MM 0
- ❏ This is you just married on Smathers Beach *(optional)*
- ❏ This is you – deciding to stay

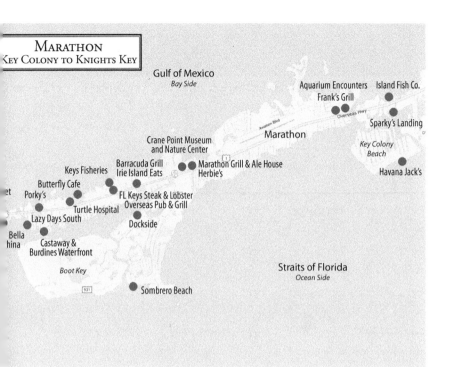

Gulf of Mexico
Bay Side

Aquarium Encounters   Island Fish Co.
Frank's Grill

Sparky's Landing

Crane Point Museum
and Nature Center   Marathon

Key Colony
Beach

Keys Fisheries   Barracuda Grill   Marathon Grill & Ale House
                    Irie Island Eats   Herbie's
Butterfly Cafe   Havana Jack's
Porky's
            FL Keys Steak & Lobster
Turtle Hospital   Overseas Pub & Grill
Lazy Days South
                    Dockside
Bella
hina   Castaway &
Burdines Waterfront

Boot Key

Straits of Florida
Ocean Side

931

Sombrero Beach

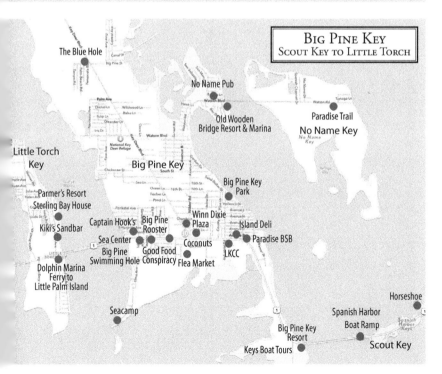

The Blue Hole

No Name Pub

Old Wooden
Bridge Resort & Marina

Paradise Trail

No Name Key

Little Torch
Key   Big Pine Key

Big Pine Key
Park

Parmer's Resort
Sterling Bay House
                                    Winn Dixie
Kiki's Sandbar   Plaza
        Captain Hook's Big Pine   Island Deli
        Sea Center   Rooster   Coconuts
                                            Paradise BSB
        Big Pine   Good Food
Dolphin Marina Swimming Hole Conspiracy Flea Market   LKCC
Ferry to
Little Palm Island

Horseshoe

Seacamp   Spanish Harbor
                                            Boat Ramp
                        Big Pine Key
                        Resort   Scout Key
                Keys Boat Tours

71

Gulf of Mexico
Bay Side

Marathon Ke

Middle Torch Key

Butterfly Cafe

No Name Pub

Little Torch   No Name Key

Pigeon Key

Sunset Grille
Isla Bella

Parmer's Resort

Kikis

Big Pine Key

Sunshine Key
RV Resort & Marina

Seven Mile Bridge

Sombrero Be

Ramrod Key

Veteran's Park
Little Duck Key

Big Pine
Rooster

Horseshoe

Ohio Key

5 Brothers Two
Boondocks
Looe Key Tiki Bar

Big Pine Key
Resort

Scout
Key

Bahia Honda State Park

Bahia Honda
Key

Little Palm
Island

Keys Boat Tours

Straits of Florida
Ocean Side

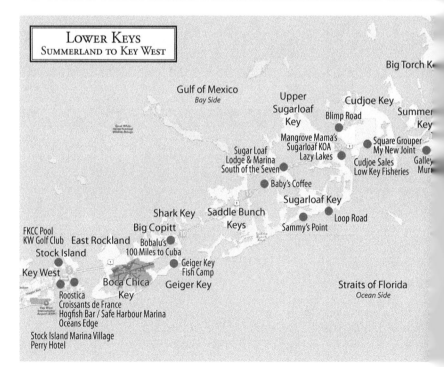

Big Torch K

Gulf of Mexico
Bay Side

Upper
Sugarloaf
Key

Cudjoe Key

Summer
Key

Blimp Road

Mangrove Mama's
Sugarloaf KOA
Lazy Lakes

Square Grouper
My New Joint

Sugar Loaf
Lodge & Marina
South of the Seven

Cudjoe Sales
Low Key Fisheries

Galley
Mur

Baby's Coffee

Sugarloaf Key

Shark Key   Saddle Bunch

Loop Road

Big Copitt

Keys

Sammy's Point

FKCC Pool
KW Golf Club   East Rockland   Bobalu's
Stock Island   100 Miles to Cuba

Geiger Key
Fish Camp

Key West

Boca Chica
Key

Geiger Key

Straits of Florida
Ocean Side

Roostica
Croissants de France
Hogfish Bar / Safe Harbour Marina
Oceans Edge

Stock Island Marina Village
Perry Hotel

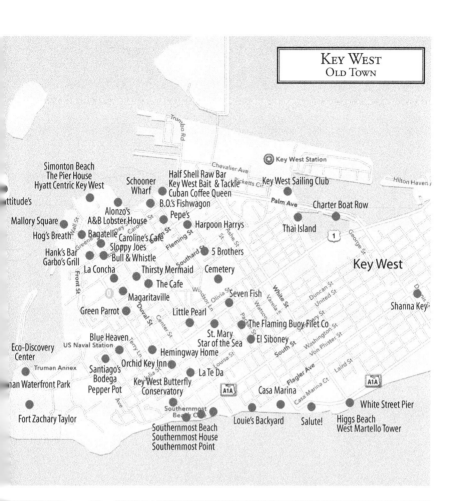

Trumbo Rd

Chevalier Ave

Key West Station

Hilton Haven

Simonton Beach
The Pier House
Hyatt Centric Key West

ttitude's

Schooner
Wharf

Half Shell Raw Bar
Key West Bait & Tackle
Cuban Coffee Queen

Ricketts Cir

Key West Sailing Club

B.O.'s Fishwagon

Palm Ave

Charter Boat Row

Alonzo's

A&B Lobster House

Pepe's

Harpoon Harrys

Thai Island

Mallory Square

Hog's Breath

Bagatelle

Caroline's Cafe

Sloppy Joes

Bull & Whistle

Fleming St

1

George St

Key West

Hank's Bar
Garbo's Grill

La Concha

5 Brothers

Wall St

Greene St

Front St

Southard St

Thirsty Mermaid

Cemetery

The Cafe

Margaritaville

Windsor Ln

Olivia St

Seven Fish

White St

Watson

Varela St

Duncan St

United St

Green Parrot

Duval St

Center St

Little Pearl

The Flaming Buoy Filet Co

Shanna Key

Blue Heaven

US Naval Station

Eco-Discovery
Center

Truman Annex

St. Mary
Star of the Sea

Hemingway Home

Terry Ln

Julia St

Louisa St

El Siboney

South St

Washington St

Von Phister St

an Waterfront Park

Santiago's
Bodega
Pepper Pot

Orchid Key Inn

Key West Butterfly
Conservatory

La Te Da

Ave

A1A

Flagler Ave

Casa Marina

Laird St

A1A

Fort Zachary Taylor

Southernmost
Beach Cafe

Southernmost Beach
Southernmost House
Southernmost Point

Louie's Backyard

Salute!

Casa Marina Ct

Higgs Beach
West Martello Tower

White Street Pier

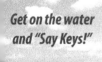

Your trip to the Keys would not be complete without trying a slice of Key Lime Pie, a specialty dessert found on the menu of most every restaurant in the Keys. If you missed it or simply want to recreate it, here is a delicious and easy recipe:

Key Lime Pie
8 SERVINGS

Pie Filling

Ingredients:
- 9" graham cracker pie shell
- 14 oz can sweetened condensed milk
- 4 egg yolks (reserve whites for meringue)
- ½ cup key lime juice (fresh if you can find it, or Nellie & Joes Key West Lime Juice)

Instructions:
Preheat oven to 350°. Blend condensed milk, egg yolks and key lime juice until smooth. Pour filling into graham cracker pie shell.

Meringue Top

Ingredients:
- 5 egg whites (use reserved whites from eggs used in pie filling + one)
- ¼ teaspoon cream of tartar
- 8 tablespoons sugar

Instructions:
Whip the egg whites at high speed with an electric mixer, until peaks have formed. Add cream of tartar. Beat in sugar, 1 tablespoon at a time; continue beating until stiff and glossy.

Spread onto pie filling, covering all of the filling to the crust edge. Make some curls or peaks. Bake for 20 to 25 minutes. Meringue should be a nice toasty light brown. Allow to stand 10 minutes. Refrigerate for a least 2 hours before serving.

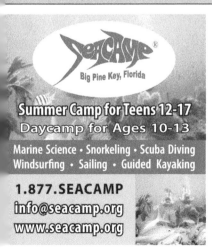
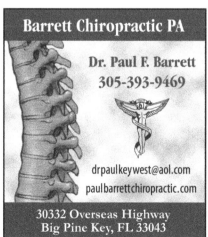

OP/PROP
OPERATION PROPAGULE

Partial proceeds from this book will go toward funding for Op/Prop, a multi-tiered effort to "prop up" our damaged mangrove islands.

Many of us know that the red mangrove tree is unique in the three mangrove species here in the Keys, in that it drops a living fruit. This fruit is known as a propagule. Propagules are living mangroves before falling off the parent tree, but still dormant in terms of taking root.

If we leave it to nature alone, it is possible our damaged islands will never recover. If we make a concerted effort, and plant propagules at assigned islands, we will perhaps manifest life – and growth, even if it takes 20+ years. The effort is larger than all of us, but try we must.

As a tour guide, I am constantly questioned about the state of our mangrove islands. The Lower Keys outside of Key West got especially hard hit. Hurricane Irma and the winds that she produced delivered perhaps a near final blow to many islands, but there is hope. The northern tip of the islands survived. The rest of the islands need major assistance. That's where we come in, to cultivate propagules – to plant.

The scientific name for the red mangrove is Rhizophora mangle, rhizo meaning root, and phora meaning, to bear or carry – in reference to the numerous prop roots growing from the trunk and branches of the mangrove. Mangle is Spanish, and means mangrove.

Crawl Key Before

Crawl Key After Irma

Once the propagule drops, it floats (for up to one year), at first horizontally, and over time, once waterlogged – vertically. During this period the roots become exposed. The propagule is now ready to secure itself in mud, sand – crevice, to plant itself and grow.

Similar to a coral lab, where men and women cultivate and then transplant coral back to the reef,we can nurture and cultivate propagule's until they are ready to grow. The idea is to plant as many propagules as we can at affected mangrove islands – and see them grow.

We miss our beautiful mangrove islands, and we want them back sooner than later. Thank you for purchasing the book and for helping us with our goal to replenish the beautiful backcountry of the Lower Keys. You can help support this effort in more ways than one at, *adoptaprop.org*.

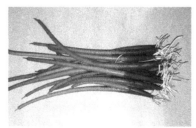

Dear Mom,

I know that this was your dream – the trip you always spoke about when we were little, but never had the time to take.

You did such a wonderful job raising us and I / we thank you. Now it's your turn.

Postcard by IslandDesign.us ©2019

POST CARD

I am sending you this ticket to Key West.

Let's explore the Lower Keys together. I'll drive. Can't wait! I love you!

XO, Allison

IslandDesign

CPSIA information can be obtained
at www.ICGtesting.com
Printed in the USA
LVHW070109180123
737306LV00008B/395